CULTURE SMART!

MEXICO

THE ESSENTIAL GUIDE TO CUSTOMS & CULTURE

RUSSELL MADDICKS

KUPERARD

"The real voyage of discovery consists not in seeking new landscapes, but in having new eyes."

Adapted from Marcel Proust, *Remembrance of Things Past.*

ISBN 978 1 78702 342 0

British Library Cataloguing in Publication Data
A CIP catalogue entry for this book is available
from the British Library

First published in Great Britain
by Kuperard, an imprint of Bravo Ltd
59 Hutton Grove, London N12 8DS
Tel: +44 (0) 20 8446 2440
www.culturesmart.co.uk
Inquiries: publicity@kuperard.co.uk

Design Bobby Birchall
Printed in Türkiye by Elma Basim

The Culture Smart! series is continuing to expand.
All Culture Smart! guides are available as e-books, and many
as audio books. For further information and latest titles visit
www.culturesmart.co.uk

ABOUT THE AUTHOR

RUSSELL MADDICKS is an award-winning, BBC-trained journalist, translator, and travel writer. A graduate in Economic and Social History from the University of Hull, England, he has spent the last twenty years traveling, living, and working in Latin America, most recently as a Regional Specialist for BBC Monitoring. He has visited Mexico on many extended trips, always finding some new and unusual facet to explore. He is also the author of *Culture Smart! Venezuela*, *Culture Smart! Ecuador* (which won the Gold Prize at the Pearl of the Pacific International Travel Journalism Awards at FITE in 2015), *Culture Smart! Cuba* (co-author), and the *Bradt Guide to Venezuela*.

CONTENTS

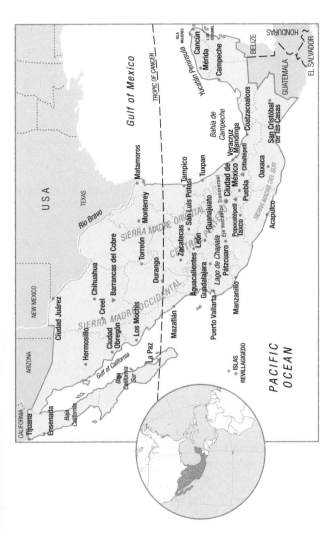

INTRODUCTION

The third-largest country in Latin America, and home to some 130 million people, Mexico is hugely diverse. It encompasses strong regional variations, major socioeconomic divisions, rural backwaters where time seems to have stopped still, and chaotic urban centers like Mexico City, one of the most densely populated, maddening, and stimulating cities in the world.

Famed for its well-preserved archaeological sites, charming cobblestoned colonial towns, and beautiful beaches along its Pacific and Atlantic coasts, Mexico is a major magnet for tourists. Whether they come to ride the Copper Canyon train in Chihuahua, watch whales in Baja California, or trek to jungle-covered Mayan temples in the deep south, visitors are increasing in number, despite negative news reports about drug gangs or spats with the US over migration. These problems, though real enough, should be seen in the wider context of a society going through far-reaching social and economic change.

This complex and fascinating country, with its tumultuous history and rich cultural and culinary legacy, is the place where European and pre-Columbian civilizations first clashed. The repercussions of the meeting in 1519 between the Spanish conquistador Hernán Cortés and the Aztec Emperor Montezuma II, and the subsequent devastation wrought by the Spanish Conquest, are still felt today and reflected in attitudes toward race and national identity.

Culture Smart! Mexico takes you beyond the usual stereotypes of spicy food, Spaghetti-Western sombreros, and mariachi music into the heart of Mexican society.

It describes the dynamics of daily life, the central importance of family, the annual cycle of Catholic feasts and fiestas, and how Mexicans socialize and meet members of the opposite sex. There is advice on how to negotiate a Mexican menu, on which delicious dishes you should try, on the differences between the local spirits tequila and mescal, and how much to tip. There's also information on traveling safely and the best transport options for exploring the country. For business travelers there are sections on Mexico's economy, the general business culture, and tips on how to succeed in the local business environment.

We go behind the scenes to meet Mexico's masked *luchadores* (wrestlers), the authors, like Octavio Paz, Juan Rulfo, and Laura Esquivel, who have laid bare the Mexican soul, and the movie directors like Alejandro González Iñárritu, Alfonso Cuarón, and Guillermo del Toro, who have helped to usher in a new golden age of Mexican cinema.

Mexican culture has remained so distinctive because of the pride that ordinary people feel in their pre-Hispanic past, their independence heroes, their unique musical traditions, and their tongue-tingling food, which is appreciated all over the world. *Culture Smart! Mexico* sets out to introduce you to the proud, spiritual, fiesta-loving, defiant, dynamic, fatalistic, food-obsessed, and creative people who call this extraordinary country home.

Official Name	Estados Unidos Mexicanos (United Mexican States)	Federal Republic of 31 States and Ciudad de México (CDMX)
Population	Approx. 130 million	
Capital City	Ciudad de México Pop. 9.2 million (capital); 22 million (metropolitan area)	
Main Cities	Guadalajara (5.3 million), Monterrey (5.2 million), Puebla (3.2 million), Tijuana (2.3 million)	
Area	761,606 sq. miles (1,972,550 sq. km)	Third-largest country in Latin America after Brazil and Argentina
Geography	Bordered by the USA to the north, and Guatemala and Belize to the south Atlantic and Pacific coasts	
Climate	Subtropical	Dry season Dec–April/May. Rainy season June–Nov. Average high 81°F (27°C) in June; low 70°F (21°C) in January
Ethnic Makeup	Mestizo (mixed-race Spanish-Indigenous) 64%; Indigenous 15%; European descent 8%; Afro-Mexican 1.6%; Asian 1%; Arab 1%; US 1.2%	

Language	Spanish	68 national languages, 63 of which are Indigenous
Religion	Roman Catholic 78%; Protestant 11%	Approx. 58,000 Jews and 8,000 Muslims
Government	Federal Republic with a President elected every six years	Two Legislative Chambers: Senate, Chamber of Deputies
Press	Main newspapers: *Reforma, La Jornada*; plus sensationalist tabloids	*Mexico Today* and *Mexico News Daily* provide English language news online.
Television	TV Azteca and Televisa produce popular telenovelas (soap operas)	Cable and Satellite widely available, and streaming services now popular
Currency	Mexican Peso ($), divided into 100 centavos	
GDP per Capita	US $9,926 (2023)	
Electricity	110 volts, 60Hz. European appliances need 2 pin round adaptors	
Internet Domain	.mx	
Telephone	International dialing code +52	City codes: Mexico City 55; Guadalajara 33; Monterrey 81; Mérida 999; Cancún 998
Time Zone	UTC/GMT −5 to −8. Daylight Saving from April to October	

CHAPTER ONE

LAND & PEOPLE

GEOGRAPHICAL SNAPSHOT

The smallest of the countries that make up North America and the third-largest Latin American country after Brazil and Argentina, Mexico covers an area of 761,610 square miles (1,972,550 sq. km)—roughly three times the size of the US state of Texas, or eight times the size of the United Kingdom. It is bordered by the Gulf of California and the Pacific Ocean to the east and the Gulf of Mexico and the Caribbean to the west, and stretches from the US states of California, Arizona, New Mexico, and Texas in the north to the Central American countries of Guatemala and Belize in the south and southeast.

The country's largest river is the Río Bravo (Rio Grande in the USA), which marks the border with Texas and flows into the Gulf of Mexico. The largest lake is Lago de Chapala, in Jalisco State, home to Mexico's largest US expat community.

The country sits on the Tropic of Cancer and its terrain is extremely diverse, with large expanses of arid scrubland

Lands End and the Arch of Cabo San Lucas in Baja California Sur.

in the northern Sonoran and Chihuahuan Deserts, temperate highlands running down the center of the country, swamps and seasonally flooded plains on the Gulf Coast, underground rivers and cenote wells in the Yucatán Peninsula, and lush rainforest in the southern state of Chiapas.

The central Mexican plateau is home to Mexico City, one of the biggest metropolitan areas in the world with an estimated population of 22 million people. The central highlands are flanked by two impressive mountain ranges—the Sierra Madre Oriental in the east and the Sierra Madre Occidental in the west, which is famous for the jagged valleys of Copper Canyon, Mexico's answer to the Grand Canyon.

In the south, the Eje Volcánico Transversal (Trans-

Ik-Kil Cenote, located in the Yucatán peninsula.

Mexican Volcanic Belt) is named for its snow-covered volcanic peaks. The smouldering cone of Popocatépetl is Mexico's second highest mountain at 17,802 feet (5,426 m) and can be clearly seen on smog-free days from Mexico City, some forty-three miles (70 km) to the northwest. The country's most active volcano, it has erupted several times in recent years.

An Aztec legend that mirrors Shakespeare's tragedy *Romeo and Juliet* states that the nearby volcano of Iztaccíhuatl (Nahuatl for "white woman") was a young maiden who fell in love with the warrior Popocatépetl and took her own life when she was falsely told he had perished in battle. The four volcanic cones of Iztaccíhuatl rise to 17,160 feet (5,230 m) and locals say they mark out the silhouette of a sleeping woman. The furious eruptions of Popocatépetl, they explain, are the rage of the brave warrior who lost his only love.

Citlaltépetl, or Pico de Orizaba—a dormant volcano—is the highest mountain in Mexico at 18,490 feet (5,636 m) and the third highest in North America after Denali (Mount McKinley) in the USA and Mount Logan in Canada.

The Trans-Mexican Volcanic Belt is also home to Mexico's rare and endangered *oyamel* (sacred fir) forests. From October to March these high-peak forests pay host to hundreds of millions of monarch butterflies (*Danaus plexippus*), which travel here on a 2,500-mile migration from Canada to overwinter. Considered one of nature's great spectacles, the monarch migration attracts a large

Sumidero cliffs at Chiapa de Corzo, Chiapas.

Monarch butterflies in Michoacan.

number of naturalists and tourists each year and the *oyamel* forests in Michoacan State are now protected within the Reserva de la Biosfera Mariposa Monarca (Monarch Butterfly Biosphere Reserve).

Mexico has the most biosphere reserves in Latin America, with forty-one of its unique and fragile ecosystems protected by UNESCO. El Vizcaino in central Baja California is Mexico's largest protected area, covering the whale calving areas of Ojo de Liebre, Laguna San Ignacio, and parts of the Gulf of California, and is one of the best places in the world to observe marine life. Famous French oceanographer and film maker Jacques Cousteau called the Gulf of California "the world's aquarium," and thousands of tourists come here each year to see gray whales, blue whales, sperm whales, and dolphins from mid-December to mid-April, which is prime whale-watching season.

In Quintana Roo State, in the south of the Yucatán peninsular, the Sian Ka'an Biosphere Reserve is a UNESCO World Heritage Site that encompasses mangroves, tropical forests, and offshore access to the Mesoamerican Reef, which is home to a richer diversity of marine life than Australia's Great Barrier Reef.

CLIMATE

Temperatures in Mexico can vary considerably, depending on location and elevation, with hot, dry deserts in the north, snow and ice in high mountain valleys, cool climes in the high central plateau, hot and humid rainforest in Chiapas, hot and sticky swamplands on the Gulf Coast, and a warm year-round climate on the coast.

The main seasons are the *temporada seca* (dry season) from December to April, which is also known as *invierno* (winter), and the *temporada de lluvias* (rainy season) from May to November, which is also known as *verano* (summer). The hottest months are May and June, and the wettest months coincide with the hurricane season from late June to November.

Temperatures in Mexico City vary a few degrees from warm daytime highs of 71.6°F (22°C) in December to 80.6°F (27°C) in June, and night-time lows of 42.8°F (6°C) in December and 53.6°F (12°C) in June.

PEOPLE

Mexico is often described as a mestizo nation, deriving from the Spanish word *mestizaje,* meaning "mixed ancestry." Some 64 percent of the population are identified as mestizo by researchers, but the country's racial reality is much more nuanced than the statistics suggest, and most people prefer to identify themselves simply as Mexicans.

The sixty-eight Amerindian Indigenous groups recognized by the state make up about 15 percent of the population, for example, but over 21.5 percent of those surveyed for the 2020 census self-identified as Indigenous. There are nearly 2 million speakers of Nahuatl, the language of the ancient Aztecs, nearly a million speakers of Yucatec Maya, half a million Zapotec speakers, and the same number of Mixtec speakers.

The inclusion of Afro-Mexicans in the 2015 census acknowledged for the first time the descendants of Mexico's African slaves. In the 2020 census over 2.5 million people identified as Black, Afro-Mexican, or of African descent.

Previously ignored and left out of Mexican history books that lionized the country's Indigenous past, Afro-Mexicans have pushed hard for recognition in recent years, especially in communities like Costa Chica, on the coast of Oaxaca, and towns like Mandinga and Mozambique, near Veracruz. Afro-pride campaigns have also highlighted the contributions of the Afro-Mexican independence heroes José María Morelos, and President Vicente Ramon Guerrero, who abolished slavery in 1829. The greatest concentration of Afro-Mexicans is in

Guerrero State, named in honor of the great general.

Mexicans still refer to Arabic people—both Christian and Muslim—as "*Turcos*" (Turks), a legacy of the period before and after the First World War when many Lebanese Christians came to Mexico from a collapsing Ottoman Empire. Although small in number (some 400,000), the Lebanese are strongly represented in business and the professions. Famous Lebanese Mexicans include the multibillionaire Carlos Slim, one of the world's richest men, and the Hollywood actress and producer Salma Hayek.

Chinese communities were established in the nineteenth century. There is a large Barrio Chino (Chinatown) in Mexico City. Another, La Chinesca, in Mexicali, boasts the highest concentration of Cantonese-style restaurants in Mexico.

Blue-eyed, blond-haired German and Dutch Mennonites have established small but culturally distinct farming communities in the states of Aguascalientes, Chihuahua, Durango, and Zacatecas. The largest Mennonite group in Latin America is to be found in Ciudad Cuauhtémoc in Chihuahua.

THE STATES OF MEXICO

Mexico is a Federal Republic with thirty-one states and, until recently, a Distrito Federal (Federal District) representing the capital city and seat of government. In 2018, the Distrito Federal, better known by its acronym DF (pronounced "day-efay"), was officially replaced by Ciudad de México (Mexico City), giving it more of the autonomous powers granted to states. The rebranding process has already started, with the city's new abbreviation CDMX widely displayed on hoardings, and taxis are being repainted pink and white to match the city's new colors. Traditionally referred to as "Chilangos" or "Defeños" (residents of DF), or irreverently as "Defectuosos" (defects), the inhabitants of the capital have now been renamed "Mexiqueños." This shouldn't be confused with "Mexiquenses," who are people from Mexico State, or "Mexicanos," which refers to Mexicans in general.

A BRIEF HISTORY

The epic, turbulent, and remarkable story of Mexico covers such a vast swathe of time that it is only possible to give a brief sketch of the arrival of the first nomadic mammoth-hunters; the rise and fall of the great civilizations of the pre-Columbian era; the conquest of the Aztecs by the Spanish; the fight for independence; foreign military interventions; the loss of territory to the USA; the Revolution; and the building of a modern democracy. (For an instant snapshot of Mexico's colorful history, there is no better place to start than Diego Rivera's magnificent History of Mexico mural that graces the staircase of the National Palace in Mexico City.)

The First Americans
The traditional theory of the peopling of the Americas suggests that bands of hunter-gatherers came across the Bering Strait from Siberia during the last ice age, some

12,000 years ago. However, the dating of recently discovered stone tools from the Chiquihuite Cave in Zacatecas State in 2017 indicate that the first people to reach Mexico may have arrived as far back as 25,000 to 30,000 years ago, while some archaeologists argue that the peopling of the Americas may go back further still, estimating a human history in the area that stretches back 45,000 years. The most complete skeleton of an early American so far discovered is a teenage girl that scientists have named Naia. Her well-preserved skull and skeleton date back 12–13,000 years and were found—alongside bones of Pleistocene mammals such as saber-tooth cats, giant ground sloths, and cave bears—in the Hoyo Negro (Black Hole) underwater cave system in the Yucatán Peninsula.

Early Americans, also known as Paleo-Indians, hunted giant mammals, such as Columbian mammoths, until these became extinct around 9,000 years ago through overhunting or climate change. The bones of some fifty mammoths have been excavated around Mexico City.

Following the domestication of corn (*Zea mays*) from a plant called *teosinte* about 10,000 years ago, several important civilizations arose in Mesoamerica (Middle America), a cultural area that extends from central Mexico to Nicaragua and Costa Rica in Central America.

Formative Period

The first major group to emerge in Mesoamerica was the Olmec, who settled in cities or ceremonial centers in San Lorenzo, La Venta, Laguna de los Cerros, and Tres Zapotes on the Gulf Coast between 1,800 and 400 BCE. They built earth pyramids to worship their gods, carved large,

Olmec Colossal Head in the ancient city of La Venta.

enigmatic stone heads of their warrior kings, practiced cranial modification to distinguish castes, traded with distant groups in Central America for jadeite and serpentine, and had a religion that incorporated strange "were-jaguars" (half human and half feline).

Sometimes described as the Mother Culture of Mesoamerica, the Olmec are also believed to have used a complex calendar based on astronomical observations and to have made blood sacrifices to their gods. Although some glyphic inscriptions survive, there is not enough early Olmec writing to provide substantial insight into their beliefs or social structures. Even their name has come to us from the later Aztecs, who called a contemporary people on the Gulf Coast Olmeca (the rubber people). A 3,000-year-old rubber ball excavated at the Olmec site of El Manati, in Veracruz, is evidence that the Olmec played the Mesoamerican ball game, a ceremonial face-off between two teams that had a ritual significance.

Pre-Classic and Classic Period

From about 150 BCE to 150 CE, at the end of the Pre-Classic period, important city-states arose, such as the Zapotec city of Monte Alban in modern-day Oaxaca and Teotihuacán in the Valley of Mexico. The Classic Period from 250 to 900 CE saw the Maya civilization reach its zenith across modern-day Mexico, Guatemala, and Honduras in city-states run by warrior chieftains such as Palenque, Uxmal, and Chichén Itzá.

Teotihuacán

At its height this imposing city of stone pyramids and ceremonial plazas was home to some 200,000 people, but a lack of hieroglyphic inscriptions to fill in the details means we know little about those who ruled here. The name comes from the Aztecs, who visited it hundreds of years after it had been burned and abandoned. They were so impressed by the monumental scale of the architecture that they called it Teotihuacán, Nahuatl for "Birthplace of the Gods." The Pyramid of the Sun is the biggest pyramid structure in the Americas, and a tunnel found in 2003 under the Pyramid of Quetzalcoatl (the Plumed Serpent) has shed new light on the religious ceremonies practiced there.

The "Birthplace of the Gods" in Teotihuacán.

The Maya

Like the city-states of Ancient Greece, the Mayan
population centers that flourished in Southern Mexico,
Honduras, and Guatemala shared a common culture,
including a huge pantheon of gods, an ancient calendar
developed from observations of the sun, the stars, and the
planets, an advanced mathematical system employing zero,
and a sophisticated hieroglyphic writing system. Warrior
kings ruled these city-states, and their stone monuments
list royal dynasties, wars of conquest, and human sacrifice.
Brightly colored murals in the Mayan city of Bonampak,
in Chiapas, show ritual bloodletting and the sacrifice of

25

captive lords. Dating to 790 CE, they mark the beginning of the end for the Maya civilization, as climate change, poor harvests, and unsustainable populations caused the main Mayan city-states to collapse.

The Post-Classic Period

One group that established itself at present-day Tula was the militaristic Toltecs, whose pyramids feature standing warriors carrying *atlatls* (spear throwers) and who established a trading empire from around 800 to 1000 CE. As yet unexplained by archaeologists, Toltec influence also appears 800 miles away in the Post-Classic architecture of the Mayan city of Chichén Itzá, including stone statues of seated warriors, called *chacmools*, and a central temple, El Castillo, dedicated to Kukulkan, the feathered serpent that the Toltecs worshipped as Quetzalcoatl. This Toltec style of building coincides with the brief resurgence of Chichén Itzá and other Mayan cities around 900 CE.

This period also saw the arrival in central Mexico of nomadic Chichimec tribes from the northern deserts. One of those tribes, the Aztecs, would go on to build the most powerful empire ever seen in Mesoamerica.

The Aztecs

Following a prophecy from Huitzilopochtli, god of the sun, fire, and human sacrifice, the Mexica tribe left their ancestral homeland in Aztlán and wandered for many years until they came across an island in Lake Texcoco and found the sign they had been seeking: an eagle perched on a cactus devouring a snake. On that spot, in 1325, they built the city of Tenochtitlán. That's the legend, at least, and the image of the eagle is enshrined in Mexico's flag.

The real story of the Mexica is of a vassal tribe to more powerful neighbors, who, over a century of fighting for others, grew powerful enough to take control of the city-states around Lake Texcoco and build their own empire. At its height, just before the Spanish conquest, this vast trading empire extended down to Nicaragua and Costa Rica. The basis of Aztec religion was sacrifice, either by ritual bloodletting or by full-on human heart extraction, because they believed that the gods of the sun, Huitzilopochtli, and rain, Tlaloc, had to be nourished with blood. War became a ritual enterprise, and death, blood, and sacrifice were exalted in elegant Aztec poems. Warriors dressed as eagles and jaguars fought so-called "flower wars" with neighboring states where the object was not to kill enemies on the battlefield but to bring back captives whose hearts would be cut out at the top of the Templo Mayor, the vast stone pyramid at the heart of Tenochtitlán.

It's easy to focus on the bloodletting that left the steps of the great pyramid sticky with gore, but the Aztec city was also a marvel of organization, home to 200,000 citizens, who were fed by an ingenious system of floating gardens called *chinampas* that can still be appreciated in the Mexico City suburb of Xochimilco.

The hierarchy of the Aztec Empire started at the top, with the emperor and the royal family—then came the priests and the warrior generals. The *pochteca* (traders) formed a middle class above craftsmen and the rest of the population, who received food and goods for working in agriculture and construction. There was no money economy: trade was carried out through barter, and goods came to Tenochtitlán as tribute from conquered states, who were able to keep their own leaders.

The Spanish Conquest

The conquest of the mighty Aztec Empire by a group of six hundred Spanish conquistadors is one of the key events in world history: a collision of the Old World with a New World in which the Europeans were victorious and stopped an advanced American civilization in its tracks. Like the conquest of the Incas in Peru, the conquest of the Aztecs hinged to some extent on the more efficient arms of the Spanish, who brought steel, horses, and cannons to the battlefield. But it was aided by the Old World diseases of smallpox and influenza that swept before the invaders, decimating local populations and sapping their ability to defend themselves. The Spanish policy of seizing the emperor was crucial at the beginning of both campaigns. In the long run it was the key alliances with disaffected tribes, providing thousands more fighters, that allowed a small band of soldiers to conquer a vast territory, although the full conquest of present-day Mexico took 150 years to complete.

Cortés and Moctezuma

In February 1519, the Spanish conquistador Hernán Cortés left the Spanish-controlled island of Cuba to explore the coast of Mexico. His first stop was the island of Cozumel, where he found a Spanish sailor, Jerónimo de Aguilar, who had been shipwrecked and had spent eight years with the local Maya. In April the Spanish defeated an Indigenous army near the Grijalva River, and Cortés was presented with a girl, called Malinalli or Malintzin, who could speak both Maya and Nahuatl, the language of the Aztecs. La Malinche, as she is known, played a key role in the conquest and had a son by Cortés, but has been vilified by later Mexican writers and historians for betraying her people and aiding the invaders.

When the Spanish arrived in modern-day Veracruz on the Gulf Coast, news of the curious strangers reached the ears of the Aztec emperor, Moctezuma II, who sent ambassadors inviting them to Tenochtitlán. The journey took three months, but by the time Cortés arrived he had fought many battles and made new alliances with local tribes.

After meeting Moctezuma, Cortés immediately took him prisoner, demanding a huge ransom for his release. Cortés then defeated a military expedition sent by the governor of Cuba, who wanted the spoils of this new land for himself.

After an Aztec revolt broke out, led by Moctezuma's younger brother Cuitláhuac, Moctezuma was killed, either by the Spanish or his own people. On June 30, 1520, "La Noche Triste" (the Night of Sorrows), as the Spaniards called it, the embattled Spanish were forced to flee the city, resulting in many of Cortes' men being killed, or sacrificed by the Aztec priests. It was the first major defeat for the Spaniards, but it came too late to save the Aztecs. On May 26, 1521, the Spanish returned with thousands of native warriors and cut off all the causeways joining the island city of Tenochtitlán to the mainland. The new emperor Cuauhtémoc put up brave resistance to a nearly three-month siege, but the Aztecs were finally brought to surrender by famine and disease and on August 13, 1521, the city fell. Cuauhtémoc was executed.

On the ruins of the Aztec capital the Spanish built Mexico City and began the conquest of the rest of the country. Wars were fought with the Chichimecs and other tribes, and new towns were founded to exploit rich seams of silver. Only the remote Maya communities who fiercely defended their southern forests were able to survive into colonial times, but eventually even they fell. Before the arrival of Cortés, an estimated 25 million Amerindians lived in the area we now know as Mexico. Within a few years, armed conquest and disease had reduced that number to a few million survivors.

The Colonial Era

The colonization of Mexico followed the pattern employed by the Spanish across the Americas. As early as 1531 a shrine was built to the Virgin of Guadalupe on the site of a temple to the Aztec Earth Mother Tonantzin. The huge cathedral that dominates the Zócalo in Mexico City was built with stone from the Templo Mayor, the toppled Aztec pyramid of Tenochtitlán—the ruins of which you can visit today, thanks to a major archaeological project. All across the country this pattern was repeated: Catholic churches were erected on top of "heathen" temples, idols were smashed, and thousands of hieroglyphic bark books were burned by overzealous priests eager to convert their new flocks.

Hundreds of towns were built on the Spanish model, haciendas brought in horses and livestock, the Indigenous population was put to work on the land or in silver mines, and Catholic missionaries carried the conversion of the Indigenous population to the wilder frontiers of what was now the Virreinato de Nueva España (Vice-Royalty of New Spain). The viceroy represented the Spanish monarch and all productive labor in the colony had one goal: the enrichment of the Spanish Crown. Trade with other countries was prohibited, even trade between neighboring Vice-Royalties. The idea was that all goods would be imported from Spain and all raw materials exported to Spain.

A colonial class structure began to develop and people were categorized into *castas,* with Spaniards from Spain at the top, and *criollos* (Spaniards born in the Americas) below them. *Mestizos*, people of Indigenous and Spanish descent, were in the middle, Amerindians came next, and Africans brought over as slaves were at the bottom.

The Cry of Independence

At the turn of the nineteenth century, strict colonial restrictions on trade and commerce had become an onerous burden for the conservative *criollo* elite, and higher taxes were imposed from Spain. The USA had revolted against British colonial rule and won its independence in 1776, and the ideas of the French Revolution circulated among more radical thinkers who longed for greater freedom. The spark came when the French emperor Napoleon Bonaparte invaded and occupied the Iberian peninsula in 1808, deposing the Spanish monarch, King Ferdinand VII.

The first cry of independence came on September 16, 1810, when at 5:00 a.m. Father Miguel Hidalgo rang the bells of his small parish church in Dolores, near Guanajuato, and called on Mexican patriots to take up arms and fight for their freedom. The words he uttered are lost to time but were along the lines of "*Mexicanos! Viva México!*" and called for an end to the government led by the *gachupines*, a term used for the Spanish. Alongside Ignacio Allende, he raised an army of 100,000 sympathizers and led them with a flag depicting the Virgin of Guadalupe, promising an end to taxes on Indigenous peasants and the abolition of slavery. After taking several towns and cities and threatening Mexico City itself, Hidalgo was captured and executed by firing squad on July 30, 1811.

In 1813 the banner of independence was taken up by José María Morelos, whose uprising was crushed in 1815. Eventually it was the *criollos* who achieved independence under the conservative Agustín de Iturbide, who took Mexico City on September 27, 1821, and then reigned as Emperor Agustín I for nearly two years before being deposed and sent into exile. On November 1, 1823, the Federal Republic of the United Mexican States was declared and enshrined in the constitution of 1824. Iturbide returned from exile in 1824 only to be arrested and sentenced to execution by firing squad. His last words were: "I die merrily, because I die among you. I die with honor, not as a traitor." Now considered one of the great heroes of Mexico, Iturbide designed the national flag.

Upheaval and War With the USA

The new nation was thrown into chaos as free-trade, secular liberals fought for power with conservatives tied to the Catholic Church. There were some thirty presidents in the fifty years following independence, with General Antonio López de Santa Anna taking the helm no less than eleven times between 1833 and 1855. This period saw Mexico lose over half its territory to the USA. Texas went first, seceding in 1836. Then, in 1846, US President James K. Polk ordered the invasion of Mexico, leading to the fall of Mexico City to US troops, and the signing of the Treaty of Guadalupe Hidalgo in 1848, which ceded New Mexico, Nevada, Utah, Arizona, Colorado, and California to the USA.

La Reforma

The humiliating defeat and loss of territory to the USA led to the exile of Santa Anna in 1854 and an attempt at reform led by Benito Juárez, a Zapotec Indian and liberal lawyer, who drafted the Constitution of 1857, enshrining the separation of Church and state and granting land rights to Indigenous peasants.

A conservative backlash led to the War of

Portrait of Benito Juárez, 1862.

the Reform, which again threw the country into turmoil, culminating in a bizarre plan hatched by conservatives in Mexico and Napoleon III to install Maximilian of Habsburg on a Mexican throne.

A Mexican Emperor

Maximilian arrived backed by French troops and declared himself Maximilian I of Mexico on April 10, 1864. A liberal at heart, he soon lost the support of his conservative backers and faced a guerrilla war from the outset from fervent followers of Benito Juárez. When the backing of Napoleon III waned in 1866, the game was up for the unwanted emperor, who was captured in Querétaro and shot by a firing squad on June 19, 1867.

Portrait of General Porifio Díaz, 1910.

Porfiriato Leads to Revolution

General Porfirio Díaz, who had fought against the French, took power in 1876 and didn't let go until he was forced into exile in 1911. Elected president seven times in a mockery of democracy, he managed to achieve a level of peace and stability in the country that allowed business, especially foreign enterprises, to thrive. However, rural peasants were forced off their lands by large landowners, and cities became known for harsh industrial conditions; this is the climate in which the seeds of the Mexican Revolution were sown.

Revolution and Chaos

A liberal landowner, Francisco I. Madero was an unlikely revolutionary, but after the presidential election was stolen from him by Porfirio Díaz he made an impassioned call to arms from exile in Texas on November 20, 1910. The simmering resentment of Mexico's oppressed peasants and workers had come to the boil and charismatic leaders emerged, like Francisco "Pancho" Villa, a former bandit from Chihuahua, and Emiliano Zapata from Morelos, who called for "*Tierra y Libertad*" (Land and Freedom). Madero became president, but the Revolution continued as faction fought faction and the country descended into anarchy. Estimates put the death toll in the ten years of the Mexican Revolution at a million people; some scholars believe it was higher. Madero was assassinated in 1913, Emiliano Zapata in 1919, and Pancho Villa in 1923.

Modern Mexico Emerges

The Constitution of February 5, 1917 marked the end of the Revolution, but it would take many years for full peace to be achieved. The short-lived Cristero War, an anti-Catholic drive by President Plutarco Elías Calles, was bloody and divisive but succeeded in delivering a secular state. One of the most important events at this time was the 1929 founding of the Partido Nacional

Revolucionario (National Revolutionary Party), which later became the Partido Revolucionario Institucional (PRI) and controlled the Mexican presidency for seventy-one years.

Mexico flourished both economically and artistically under President Lázaro Cárdenas, who delivered on land and labor reforms and nationalized the oil industry in 1938. Muralists like Diego Rivera, David Alfaro Siqueiros, and José Clemente Orozco helped to shape this new Mexican pride, rooted in an indigenous past and revolutionary struggle.

Stability and Growth

From the 1940s to the 1960s, booming oil wealth and an emerging manufacturing industry based in Mexico City, Monterrey, and along the US border helped to fund public works and ambitious housing projects. Throughout this process, political stability was provided by the de-facto one-party state run by the monolithic PRI, which Peruvian novelist Mario Vargas Llosa dubbed the "the perfect dictatorship." Rapid urbanization also saw shanty towns appear as people moved to the big cities in search of work.

The Tlatelolco Massacre

In 1968, students inspired by the May riots in Paris took to the streets to air their grievances against the PRI government of Gustavo Díaz Ordaz. With the opening of the Olympic Games in Mexico City imminent, the government led a harsh crackdown to clear the streets of protesters. On October 2, unarmed students protesting at the Three Cultures Square in the Tlatelolco housing complex were attacked by soldiers with fixed bayonets backed up by tanks. Some estimates put the number of people killed as high as 3,000, sparking international outrage, but the Tlatelolco Massacre, as it came to be called, was never properly investigated under the PRI; even today the truth has yet to emerge.

NAFTA, the Zapatistas, and the PRI

When Carlos Salinas de Gortari became president in 1988 he embarked on a massive privatization program to stimulate the economy, stopping short of opening up the oil industry. The culmination of this economic overhaul came in 1994, when Mexico signed up to the North American Free Trade Agreement (NAFTA), essentially opening its market to goods from the USA and Canada. The result was initially catastrophic for Mexican farmers, prompting increased tension in rural areas and a spike in Mexican migrants seeking work in the US, both legally and illegally.

In rural Chiapas, the poorest state in Mexico, the reaction to NAFTA was an armed uprising by the Zapatista Army of National Liberation (ELZN), a group of intellectual radicals and Indigenous peasant farmers inspired by the ideals of Emiliano Zapata. On New Year's Day 1994 the group seized control of San Cristóbal de las Casas, sparking immediate interest from news organizations in their mysterious leader, Subcomandante Marcos, who wore a balaclava to conceal his identity (much like a *lucha libre* superhero), and smoked a pipe like a university academic. International sympathy for the Zapatistas and the intense media spotlight were likely key factors that stopped the army from responding with more brutal repression, but the situation ended in 1995 in an uneasy ceasefire. This left the Zapatistas unmolested in their autonomous communities but with few of their demands met.

The effects of NAFTA have also impacted the PRI. In 2000 the PRI's seven-decade hold on power was finally broken with the election of President Vicente Fox of the Partido Acción Nacional (PAN). The pattern continued in 2006 with the election of President Felipe Calderón,

also from PAN, who made a game-changing decision to declare war on Mexico's drug cartels, resulting in a huge increase in cartel-related violence and deaths as drug gangs militarized their own operations. Some estimates put the death toll in Mexico's war on drugs during the period from 2006 to 2012 as high as 50–60,000.

Zapatista leader Subcomandante Marcos in Chiapas.

The election of Enrique Peña Nieto in 2012 marked the return of a PRI president, but little changed in the strategy to tackle the growing violence of the cartels. Reminiscent of the Tlatelolco Massacre, the involvement of local authorities in the disappearance and probable massacre of forty-three students in Iguala on the night of September 26, 2014 prompted protests across the country and calls for an end to corruption and impunity.

The AMLO Era

A career politician from Tepetitán in Tabasco State, Andrés Manuel López Obrador was elected president in 2018 in a landslide victory that demonstrated voters' rejection of Mexico's two main parties, the PRI and PAN. It was his third run for the presidency, and he led his own party, the populist, center-left Movimiento Regeneración Nacional, or Morena (which intentionally also means "brown-skinned" in Spanish).

Making his mark in politics as the head of government of the federal district between 2000 to 2005, Amlo worked closely with the billionaire businessman Carlos Slim to clean up and restore the city's historic downtown area, and gained huge popular support by introducing pensions, scholarships, and social programs aimed at the most disadvantaged.

As president, AMLO pledged a "Fourth Transformation" (Cuarta Transformación) of politics and society following the Mexican War of Independence (1810–1821), the Reform War (1858–1861), and the Mexican Revolution (1910–1917). The key elements of T4, as it's known, included cracking down on widespread

Andrés Manuel López Obrador in 2017.

corruption, gutting a bloated bureaucracy, and tackling historical inequality in Mexican society. Progress on these key issues has been slow, and was seriously impacted by the Covid-19 pandemic that took center stage for a frantic two years. In general, while social and educational programs focusing on the poorest sectors of society pleased AMLO's supporters, there has been little action to tackle corruption.

He has also worked closely with the armed forces, putting the military in charge of curtailing the activities of drug cartels and crime groups, but also putting them in charge of operating ports, airports, and the construction of the Tren Maya project in Chiapas and the Yucatán Peninsula.

For those who have benefited from his focus on "Mexico first," which he refers to as Mexicanismo, and his man-of-the-people style, he has inspired huge devotion, but also polarization.

With reelection no longer an option under the Constitution of Mexico, many are looking to fellow Morena politician Claudia Sheinbaum Pardo—the head of government of Mexico City—to continue AMLO's state reforms. If elected, she would become Mexico's first female president.

GOVERNMENT

Mexico is a Federal Republic with thirty-one states and Ciudad de México (Mexico City), a new Federal entity representing the seat of government that replaces the Distrito Federal (DF). Voting in elections is mandatory and there is universal suffrage for all Mexicans over the age of eighteen.

The division of powers in Mexico is similar to the US system. The legislative branch is divided into a Senate, with 128 senators elected every six years, and a Chamber of Deputies, with 500 members elected every three years.

The executive branch is led by the president, who is the head of state and government and the Supreme Commander of the armed forces. The president can appoint a cabinet, the attorney general, military chiefs, and Supreme Court Justices.

Elections for president are held every six years and presidents can serve only one term. This restriction on reelection, known as the *sexenio,* was introduced to avoid a repetition of the "Santa Anna Age," when the Mexican general Antonio López de Santa Anna dominated politics and was president eleven times over a forty-year period, and the twenty-six years of the "Porfiriato," when Porfirio Díaz ruled the country.

The *sexenio* had little effect, however, in stopping the Partido Revolucionario Institucional (PRI) from running Mexico like a one-party state for seventy-one years (1929–2000), as outgoing presidents would simply name their successor.

State governors are also elected, serving a single six-year term, and state assemblies have the power to levy local taxes. The states have their own courts with the power to rule on local cases, but appeals can be taken to the Supreme Court, the highest court in the land.

NATIONAL SYMBOLS

A source of great pride for Mexicans is the national flag, a vertical tricolor of green, white, and red, in use since the nineteenth-century wars of independence. The national coat of arms that appears in the center of the flag invokes the Aztec legend of the founding of Tenochtitlán and shows an eagle, with a snake held in one of its talons, perched on a prickly pear cactus growing from a rock in a lake. (See page 26 for more on the Aztec legend.)

National anthem: "Mexicanos, al Grito de Guerra" ("Mexicans, at the Cry of War") by Francisco González Bocanegra, music by Jaime Nunó.
National bird: Quebrantahuesos Mexicano (Northern Crested Caracara).
National flower: Dahlia (Dahlia pinnata).
National tree: Ahuehuete (Montezuma Cypress).

THE ECONOMY

One of the most important trade deals Mexico ever signed was the North American Free Trade Agreement (NAFTA) with the US and Canada in 1994. That deal was reaffirmed in 2018 under the renegotiated terms of the United States-Mexico-Canada Agreement (USMCA), which came into effect in 2020. Pre-NAFTA, Mexico was dependent on oil for some 80 percent of its foreign currency earnings. Oil now represents only about 10 percent of total export earnings, but is an important source of government revenue through the state-owned oil company Pemex.

NAFTA led to the diversification of the economy and the rapid growth of the manufacturing industry, especially the large-scale assembly plants, or *maquiladoras*, along the border with the USA.

Apart from automobiles and domestic goods, Mexico has developed an important electronics industry and is expanding into aerospace. While the country has signed free trade agreements with forty-six countries, 80 percent of exports go to the USA, now under the revised USMCA treaty.

Raw materials and agricultural goods play a lesser role in the economy than they did pre-NAFTA, but Mexico continues to be the world's top producer of silver and avocados, and supplies 97 percent of the limes consumed in the US.

Meanwhile, an increasingly diverse and sophisticated service sector catering to Mexico's growing middle class is attracting ever greater foreign investment, especially in financial services.

In 2022, Mexico's GDP was US $1,293 trillion, reflecting the strength of its diversified economy, which includes the oil sector, remittances from Mexicans in the USA, exports, agriculture, mining, tourism, and industrial activity. Remittances from Mexicans working in the USA continue to increase, and, although figures vary, they are estimated at some US $60 billion.

Tourism has become a significant generator of income and jobs and today, Mexico is one of the top ten most popular destinations in the world, according to the UN's World Tourism Organization. Attractions like the Mayan pyramids of Yucatán, the museums of Mexico City, the white-sand beaches of Cancún, and the magnificent whale watching to be had in Baja California have all helped to attract a steadily rising number of visitors. In 2022, Mexico received over 36 million tourists, which represented a successful return to pre-Covid numbers.

The majority of visitors to Mexico come from the USA, either as tourists or to start a new life—today more than 1.6 million Americans have made Mexico their home. US expats are attracted by the warm weather, the proximity to family and friends back home, a lower cost of living, and the country's strong cultural heritage, colonial cities, and delicious cuisine (more on that in Chapter 6).

COVID-19

Mexico confirmed its first cases of Covid-19 at the end of February 2020, when it was announced that two men in Mexico City and another from Sinaloa who had returned from Italy had tested positive for the virus. The authorities in Mexico City responded by closing all bars, nightclubs, movie theaters, and museums, but it was not until the end of March, when cases topped 1,000, that a national emergency was declared.

Initially, the emphasis was on individual responsibility and social distancing, as illustrated by a popular public health campaign featuring a female superhero called Susana Distancia—"*su sana distancia*" means "a healthy distance"—who reminded people to keep a safe distance of 2 meters (about 6 feet) to stop the spread of the virus.

Arguing that a lockdown would hit the poorest hardest, President Andrés Manuel López Obrador kept the country largely open, with individual states and Mexico City setting their own regulations and restrictions as local cases spiked.

For foreign travelers, even while the USA closed the border with Mexico for all but essential crossings, Mexico remained open with few restrictions beyond mask wearing on public transport and in public spaces, and no need for vaccinations or a negative Covid-19 test to enter the country, bringing a large number of US and Canadian tourists to Cancún and the resorts along the Riviera Maya.

In December 2021 Mexico became the first Latin American nation to administer a Covid-19 vaccine, relying initially on donations from the US and then on a mixed bag of vaccines from Europe, Russia, and China. Despite a slow start, by December 2022, 77 percent of the population had been vaccinated and Mexico was producing its own doses of the AstraZeneca vaccine, providing vaccine shots to Belize, Bolivia, El Salvador, Guatemala, Honduras, and Paraguay.

CHAPTER TWO

VALUES & ATTITUDES

Given the many distinct regions of Mexico—each with its own customs, food, and music—and the huge disparities between the rich cosmopolitan elite, the growing middle class, and the many Mexicans who struggle from day to day to make ends meet, it's difficult to make generalizations about the people of Mexico. Only a short period of travel in the country, or a visit to one of the many Indigenous groups that live very distinct lives from the mainstream, is enough to conclude that there is not one Mexico but many. Yet, despite all the differences, there are values and beliefs that serve to unite Mexicans across the social divide, such as the belief in the importance of family, religion, a deep attachment to national traditions like Day of the Dead, *lucha libre*, and the mariachi music that is played at weddings and funerals, as well as an unshakeable belief that Mexican food is the best in the world. It is some of these that we shall unpack in this chapter.

RELIGION

The Roman Catholic Church has done much to shape beliefs and attitudes in Mexico since Christianity was imposed on the population in the sixteenth century, and its influence continues to be strong.

Mexico is the country with the second highest number of Catholics after Brazil, and despite congregations falling from a high in 1950 of some 98 percent of the population, 77 percent of Mexicans still identify as Catholic today. Religious festivities and Saints' Days continue to dominate the calendar, and life for the majority follows a cycle of baptisms, first communions, weddings, and funerals.

One reason for the success of Catholicism is due to the pragmatism of the Jesuit and Franciscan monks who led conversions and allowed Indigenous Mexicans to incorporate their traditional beliefs into their new form of worship, like the adoration of the Virgin of Guadalupe that incorporates elements of the worship of Tonantzin, known to the Aztecs as the Great Mother, or folk festivals held on Catholic feast days that preserve pre-Columbian beliefs, such as Día de Muertos (Day of the Dead).

Despite this, the rise of Protestant Evangelical and Pentecostal groups has caused a decline in the number of Catholics, often in marginalized areas of the country and among Indigenous groups. About 11 percent of Mexicans indicated that they were Protestant or Evangelical in the 2020 Census.

In line with other countries in the region, in Mexico there has been a rise in those who don't identify with any religion at all.

There are also small but significant Jewish communities in Mexico City and Guadalajara, with Ashkenazim from Russia, Poland, Germany, and other parts of Europe, and Sephardim, mostly from Italy and Syria.

FAMILY VALUES

Generally built around a strong mother figure, the family is hugely important to Mexicans. Few families are as large as they used to be, when a couple had seven or eight children, but the tradition of the extended family persists, with several generations often living under one roof or in close proximity. Older people are respected and are generally looked after by their families rather than going into residential homes to see out their last days.

Children are doted on and involved in social gatherings from an early age. Their birthday parties will involve several generations of the family and take place at home or in a park with a barbecue or picnic and the obligatory *piñata* full of sweets, but they are first and foremost family events, to be enjoyed as much by the adults as the kids. Mexican children grow up to be confident, if a little spoiled, but tend not to have an attitude that leaves them unable to communicate or have fun with anybody but other teenagers.

The concept of young people leaving the family home at eighteen to study or live alone as they do in the US or UK is still alien to most Mexicans, and they generally stay at home until they marry or possibly migrate for work. This is partly for economic reasons but also because life is easier in an extended family, as long as everybody gets on, especially for young men, who are rarely expected to cook or clean, are not often asked to contribute financially, and have plenty of time to socialize with friends. For those who do migrate for work, there is a round of birthdays, weddings, and holidays to keep families in close contact and maintain ties.

Poverty, or the absence of a father who might have several children with different partners, can cause families to break up, and it's not unusual for children to be raised by grandparents or aunts, or even relatives living far away in the US. In most cases, people will try to find a solution within the family before going to outside agencies.

Where women with young children have to work, it's typical for the grandparents to take over child minding, although well-off Mexicans may employ nannies and send their children to nurseries. The poorest single mothers are often forced to take their babies with them to informal jobs; you see them with their babies strapped to their backs, selling food from street stalls or hawking newspapers and snacks on the streets or on buses. For some children, poverty and family breakup can lead to a dangerous life on the streets, but the Mexican authorities have done much in recent years to provide solutions for street kids.

PRIDE, HONOR, AND *MACHISMO*

Machismo is not unique to Mexico. Most Latin American countries have a macho stereotype to which many men still aspire: a strong, decisive, and stoic individual who is unafraid of danger and quick to defend any slight against his family or country, no matter the odds.

On the positive side, old-school macho men are expected to be generous and show respect to women, especially mothers and grandmothers. On the downside, they can be aggressive and demanding, and can take rejection badly.

Piropos (romantic compliments) are a throwback to the days when men would write love poetry to their *amores*. Mexican men are still romantic (just listen to the love songs in the Mexican charts), but overly sexual *piropos*—like wolf whistles—come across as crude and closer to harassment. Casual sexism is everywhere, from the home, where boys are allowed to play while girls are expected to help in the kitchen, to the workplace, where women are expected to dress up and look good if they want to get ahead.

The flip side of *machismo* is matriarchy, and mothers and grandmothers tend to rule the roost at home, bringing up the children, managing the domestic budget, and holding down a job at the same time.

Tequila Tears

Lilting laments to lost love, Mexico's sad mariachi songs are sure-fire tear-jerkers—the musical equivalent of chopping onions for its macho men. The image of a despondent drinker dripping salty tears into his shot glass as he slumps on the bar of a *cantina* is immortalized in the song "Ella" (She) by José Alfredo Jiménez: "I wanted to forget in the style of Jalisco, but those mariachis and that tequila made me cry."

LGBTQ IN A MACHO SOCIETY

While macho culture and the disapproval of the Catholic Church held back gay rights across the country in the past, things are changing fast. Government support, new laws, and progressive social media campaigns have helped to raise awareness of gay and transgender issues and establish greater levels of acceptance in Mexican society as a whole.

Pioneering out-and-proud characters like the flamboyant wrestling star Cassandro, known as the Liberace of Lucha Libre, have led the way to greater acceptance for the LGBTQ community. A 2023 movie called *Cassandro* about the wrestler's life saw Mexico's most famous international star Gael Garcia Bernal give an intimate behind-the-scenes portrayal of Cassandro's loves and losses.

Trans pioneers include the remarkable Amelio Robles Ávila (3 November 1889–9 December 1984), a hero of the Mexican Revolution who rose to the rank of colonel and lived openly as a man from the age of twenty-four until his death aged ninety-five.

In Oaxaca, the Zapotec people have embraced trans women since ancient times, with a third sex category known as Muxe, men who dress as women and assume traditionally female roles in society.

The biggest expression of LGBTQ liberation is at annual events like Gay Pride, held in June, which is celebrated with processions in Mexico City, most major cities, and beach resorts. The week-long Pride party held in May in the resort of Puerto Vallarta is one of the leading LGBTQ celebrations in Latin America.

Mexico City has led the way on rights, legalizing same-sex marriage in 2009 and holding mass weddings in the city's main square, the Zócalo, attended by LGBTQ couples from around the country. A Supreme Court decision in 2015 ruled that it was unconstitutional to refuse same-sex marriages but it was not until October 2022, when Mexico's northeastern state of Tamaulipas finally recognized same-sex marriage, that it became legal throughout the country. Welcoming the vote in Tamaulipas, President of the Supreme Court of Justice Arturo Zaldívar posted on Twitter: "The whole country shines with a huge rainbow. Live the dignity and rights of all people. Love is love."

While there are still challenges that the gay and trans communities face in regards to discrimination, LGBTQ travelers in Mexico will find a friendly welcome in the country's main destinations and will be unlikely to encounter problems visiting smaller, rural towns in the interior.

DISTRUST OF AUTHORITIES

An anti-establishment tendency runs deep in Mexico's veins. Some scholars trace this lawless streak back to the Spanish Conquest when the only protest open to the subjugated Aztecs and other Indigenous Mexicans was to ignore or subvert—where possible—the laws of their foreign overlords. This tendency was strengthened by the many revolts and uprisings during the War of Independence, the unrest caused by the French and US invasions, the long chaos of the Mexican revolution, and the seventy-year "perfect dictatorship" under the PRI.

Local attitudes toward the rule of law is perhaps best

summed in the saying "*El que no tranza, no avanza,*" which translates roughly as "If you don't cheat, you don't get ahead." The line was first used in the 1999 satirical movie *La ley de Herodes* that portrays the corrosive effects of political corruption on Mexican society.

Widespread disdain for the politicians and institutions tasked with implementing the law and governance, such as police, the courts, and government officials, has resulted in a beat-the-system mentality; people rely on their families and close friends for help rather than on the authorities.

In rural areas and in Indigenous communities, distrust of central government has led to protest movements like the 1994 Zapatista uprising in Chiapas, which continues to this day, and the more recent phenomenon of vigilante groups that have formed to protect their towns and villages against the activities of local drug cartels.

ATTITUDES TOWARD RACE

The Spanish arrived in the New World shortly after the final push to rid Spain of the Moors following eight hundred years of Muslim rule. It was a time of great intolerance toward other faiths and saw the rise of the feared Spanish Inquisition to root out heresy. In the same year that Christopher Columbus set sail on his epic voyage, the Jews and Muslims of Spain were being forced to convert to Christianity or flee for their lives.

After conquering the Aztecs and other Indigenous kingdoms, the Spanish created the rigid hierarchy known as the *casta* system. At the top were the Spanish-born *peninsulares*, followed by the *criollos* (Creoles, or locally born people of Spanish descent), *mestizos* (people of mixed Spanish and Indigenous backgrounds), *indios* (Indigenous people), and black slaves from Africa.

Since independence, Mexico has been through several periods where the country's Indigenous heritage has been celebrated, especially in the 1920s and '30s when artists, writers, and archaeologists began to restore national pride in the country's pre-Hispanic past. However, despite huge advances in social mobility, people are often still judged by their skin color.

Terms like "*negro*" (black) and "*Indio*" (Indian) are often used affectionately among family members, especially in the dimunitive, but would be considered offensive if used by strangers. Common racism manifests in phrases like "*Hay que mejorar la raza,*" ("You have to improve the race,") suggesting that a lighter-skinned partner is preferable.

As discussed, until 2015 there was no box in the national census for "Black" or "African" and only after sustained demands from activists was a question about Black ethnicity included. Once it was, 1.4 million Mexicans identified as Black or of African descent, rising to 2.6 million in 2020. An Afro-pride movement that emerged in the Afro-Mexican communities of Veracruz, Guerrero, and Oaxaca has helped highlight the lack of representation of Mexico's Black population in the media, and elsewhere, prompting calls for change.

Leading the movement for a more inclusive society are figures like Yalitza Aparicio, an Indigenous preschool teacher from Oaxaca who played the role of the maid Cleo in director Alfonso Cuarón's award-winning 2018 movie *Roma*.

Aparicio was the first Indigenous American woman to receive a Best Actress nomination at the Oscars and was subsequently named a UNESCO Goodwill Ambassador for Indigenous Peoples. *TIME* magazine named her one of the 100 most influential people in the world.

Another actor pushing hard for change is Tenoch Huerta, who played Namor in the 2022 Mayan-inspired Black Panther sequel *Wakanda Forever*. Huerta's 2022 book *Orgullo Prieto* (Dark-Skinned Pride) challenges the argument that *"Somos todos mestizos"* ("We are all mixed race") and calls for an end to the racism that holds back Black, brown, and Indigenous Mexicans.

LIVING FOR THE MOMENT

In a society where the uncertainties of life can easily throw a curveball at a person's best-laid plans and many people survive day to day on what they can make in the informal economy, it's perhaps not surprising that people have developed an attitude that prioritises living for the moment. In rural communities and in the poorer *barrios* of Mexico's cities, the monotony of the daily grind is broken up only by the annual cycle of family get-togethers, religious celebrations, and national holidays, and people make sure they make the most of these events.

There's a popular Mexican phrase that expresses this sentiment: *"Si con el cántaro sudas, ¿qué harías con el chochocol?"* ("If you sweat over a small jar, what would you do for a big jar?") What it means is: life can be hard, so don't sweat the small stuff. Instead, try to make the most of the hand that fate has dealt you.

This idea can also be seen reflected in people's saving habits, where instead of saving, many Mexicans will spend liberally and instead opt to use the *tanda* or *cundina* system, an informal savings or loan club, to pay for a *quinceañera* celebration or a sudden emergency that may arise.

Historic Fatalism

Young Mexicans may not recognize themselves in this portrayal, but if there is one characteristic that stands out from historical descriptions of the Mexican people, it is melancholic fatalism: a resignation that the worst is likely to happen, that some inevitable doom is just around the corner, and that, overall, life is hard and pleasure fleeting. Historian Salvador de Madariaga argued that this fatalistic outlook is rooted in Mexico's past and the Spanish Conquest of the Aztecs, writing: "Every day, within the soul of every Mexican, Moctezuma dies and Cuauhtémoc is hanged."

CLASS DIVISIONS

There are sharp social divisions within Mexico. The country is home to a small handful of billionaires while 43 percent of Mexicans live below the poverty line, 8 percent live in extreme poverty, and nearly 60 percent work precarious hand-to-mouth jobs in the informal sector.

In 2022, the Economic Commission for Latin America and the Caribbean (ECLAC) ranked Mexico as the fifth poorest country in the region and warned that poverty was increasing in the country due to inflation.

A slowly growing middle class was also badly hit by the economic effects of the Covid-19 pandemic, shrinking from 53.5 million people in 2018 to 47.5 million in 2020, according to the Mexican statistics agency INEGI.

It's only in the big cities that you find a sizable middle class. In Mexico City, nearly 58 percent of the population were middle class in 2022, while in the states of Oaxaca, Guerrero, and Chiapas it was only 6 percent. In part this is because in rural areas, where agricultural work is poorly paid, the class divisions of the old hacienda system still persist, with a rich *patrón* (boss) and his family living large on the family estate while the workers struggle to make ends meet.

Indigenous Mexicans are among the poorest in society, and only 3 percent of Mexicans who speak Indigenous languages are defined as middle class.

Much of the migration to the big cities and to the US is fueled by rural poverty and the desire for a better life. One of the problems holding back social progress is the dropout rate in schools. Although education is free and open to all, about 18 percent of Mexican children between the ages of 15 and 19 do not receive high school education, according to data from the Organization for Economic Cooperation and Development (OECD). Many of those who drop out of education do so to help their families financially, especially in the informal sector.

MEXICO AND THE USA

The nineteenth-century Mexican president Porfirio Díaz once said, "Poor Mexico, so far from God and so close to the United States." His words sum up the often difficult relationship between Mexico and its northern neighbor, which more than once has descended into armed conflict and between 1846 and 1848 resulted in the loss of nearly half of Mexico's territory.

In many ways the conflict between the two countries is a fight for the survival of Mexican culture in a world where American culture predominates. Mexicans may be happy to enjoy the benefits when it comes to shopping at Walmart or any of the other US chains you find in Mexico, but they don't want to lose their street markets or their culinary traditions. It's also about national pride and not being bullied or treated as second-class by a more powerful neighbor.

Since the presidency of Barack Obama, Mexican attitudes to the US have steadily improved, especially among the young. But it only took an inflammatory statement by presidential aspirant Donald Trump in 2016 to ignite a fierce storm of protest when he described Mexicans as rapists and drug dealers and said that he wanted to build a wall along the border to keep them out. Mexicans responded to Trump in their very own way, with as much satire as anger, and gleefully made *piñata* of the tousle-haired tycoon for kids to smash, and huge papier-mâché figures to be burned at carnivals.

By and large, visiting Americans experience no animosity in Mexico, and more than 1.6 million US citizens have set up home south of the border. Most people's experience, regardless of where they're from, is that if they show respect for Mexico and its culture, and take the time to learn a few words of local Spanish, Mexicans will respond with the great warmth and hospitality for which they are famous.

The Migrant Experience

So many families in Mexico are affected by migration to the US that it is no surprise that there are strong feelings about the issue, particularly about the treatment of Mexicans who have made the journey across the border, either legally or illegally. Apart from the 38 million US citizens who identify as Mexican Americans, there are roughly 5 million Mexicans working legally in the US and an estimated 6 million living and working without formal papers. The main reason for migration is economic: a chance to get a better-paid job and save up for a better life back home.

Crossing the border illegally is fraught with danger, involving paid *coyotes* or *polleros* (people-smugglers) and a long trek through a hot desert that can be fatal to those not properly prepared and guided. Those who make it to the US and find a job can send money home to their families, but life for undocumented migrants is difficult: they risk arrest and deportation, have to work the lowest-paid and most menial jobs, and often go many years without seeing their families. Nevertheless, for many Mexicans, the employment opportunities in the US, however badly paid, represent an improvement on the poorer prospects available back home.

The increasing tensions on the border due to drug trafficking, anti-migrant vigilante groups, and the human rights abuses of Mexicans and Central American migrants by unscrupulous *polleros* are daily topics of news in Mexico.

ATTITUDES TOWARD FOREIGNERS

Few Mexicans have an opportunity to travel outside their own country, except to the US or the Caribbean, and, as a result attitudes to foreigners can seem parochial and old-fashioned, sometimes falling into simplistic stereotypes. For example, as we've seen, people from the Middle East and other Muslim countries are all lumped together as "Turkos"—a legacy of the days of the Ottoman Empire when Lebanese, Syrian, and Palestinian immigrants came to Mexico with Turkish papers.

East Asians are also lumped together in popular speech as *chinos* (Chinese), no matter if they come from Japan, Vietnam, or Korea. A typical nickname for anybody of East Asian descent (or who has Indigenous Mexican features) is El Chino or La China, often using the diminutive form *chinito* or *chinita*.

Mexicans are genuinely interested to meet foreign visitors and will try out their English—and put your Spanish to the test—to find out more about you and your country, especially about the food you eat, how much people earn, and what the weather's like. These are great conversation starters and will generally lead to questions about your opinions of Mexico. Keep conversations light and stick to positive impressions, and you may make a friend.

You may find that people stare at you on public transport or in the street for longer than you would expect at home. Don't be alarmed; it's only curiosity.

CHAPTER THREE

CUSTOMS & TRADITIONS

Mexico's annual calendar includes a dizzying whirl of religious festivals, carnivals, and national commemorations, and you can rest assured that on any given day at least one small town somewhere will be decked out in colorful bunting with locals preparing to party.

The majority of these festivals are linked to the calendar of Catholic religious observances brought from Spain by the conquistadors. Following the fall of the Aztec capital Tenochtitlán, Spanish priests zealously imposed Roman Catholicism on the Indigenous people they subjugated, introducing a cycle of moveable feasts and saints' days into the mestizo melting pot of conquest. However, travel around and you will find countless vestiges of pre-Hispanic belief and ritual conserved in the country's colorful celebrations.

Mexico's tumultuous history is also remembered through the year, with the celebration of important dates such as the Grito de Dolores (Cry of Dolores), marking Padre Miguel Hidalgo's momentous 1810 call for Mexican independence from Spain.

Joyous Explosions

Mexico's most famous man of letters, poet Octavio Paz, wrote that the country's many festivals are like a pressure valve, making life bearable for Mexico's poor and downtrodden. "Our fiestas are explosions," he wrote. "There is nothing so joyous as a Mexican fiesta, but there is also nothing so sorrowful. Life and death, joy and sorrow, music and mere noise are united."

FESTIVALS AND HOLIDAYS

Mexicans love to party, and take their festivals very seriously, with newspapers publishing the upcoming holidays at the start of the year so that families can start to plan their vacations. There are several types of holiday throughout the year. Días Feriados, also known as Días de Asueto, are statutory public holidays, where workers get a day off, or extra pay for working. Civic holidays, such as Día de la Bandera (Flag Day), are celebrated nationally but don't include a mandatory day off (although some local government offices close).

Some religious holidays, such as Carnaval (Carnival) and Semana Santa (Easter), are movable feasts that fall on different dates each year and can go on for over a week. Others, such as Día de Muertos (Day of the Dead, November 2) fall on fixed dates when banks and government offices are generally closed, but may also be extended over several days.

Where possible, it's best to avoid travel at peak holiday times or during local festivals as heavy traffic can make transportation difficult. If you do plan to participate, arrange your transportation and accommodation well in advance.

PUBLIC HOLIDAYS

January 1 Año Nuevo (New Year's Day)

First Monday in February Día de la Constitución (Constitution Day)

Third Monday in March Benito Juárez's birthday

March–April Jueves Santo (Maundy Thursday)

Viernes Santo (Good Friday)

Semana Santa (Easter)

May 1 Día del Trabajo (Labor Day)

September 16 Día de la Independencia (Independence Day)

Third Monday in November Día de la Revolución (Revolution Day)

December 25 Navidad (Christmas Day)

THE FESTIVAL CALENDAR

January 1: Año Nuevo
New Year's Eve is traditionally celebrated at home with music, dancing, drinking, and a big family meal, much like Christmas dinner. *Bacalao* (salted cod) and *pavo*

(turkey) are typically served at this time of year, and *pozole* (hominy stew made with pork or chicken) is also popular. The celebrations culminate with a glass of sparkling wine or cider and twelve grapes, which are eaten during the twelve chimes of midnight. New Year rituals include sweeping the house to get rid of bad luck, putting on new clothes to start afresh, taking a suitcase into the street to increase the chances of travel, and wearing colored underwear (red for love, yellow for money, and white for peace and health). The night ends with a bang, as fireworks fill the skies and people party into the early hours.

January 6: El Día de Reyes
Called Epiphany in English, this day celebrates the arrival of the Three Kings, Caspar, Melchior, and Balthasar, in Bethlehem with gifts of gold, frankincense, and myrrh for the baby Jesus. Many Mexican children still get their presents on this day rather than at Christmas.

February 14: Día de San Valentín
Valentine's Day isn't just about anonymous love letters, flowers, chocolates, romantic dinners, and mariachi serenades. It's also known as Día de la Amistad (Friendship Day), and many Mexicans will also celebrate the day with friends.

February 24: Día de la Bandera de México
Mexican Flag Day celebrates the day in 1821 that Agustín de Iturbide unfurled the tricolor flag for the first time, with a green stripe representing hope, white for unity, and a red stripe symbolizing the blood spilled by Mexico's

A SWEET TRADITION FOR THE THREE KINGS

Rosca de reyes is a sweet oval bread with a hole in the center that represents a crown, with dried fruit for the encrusted jewels and a small figure of the Baby Jesus baked into it. Traditionally, it is shared with friends and family on January 6, the Día de los Reyes (Three Kings' Day). The *rosca* is typically served with a cup of hot chocolate and *tamales*. Everybody waits to see who will get the slice containing the Baby Jesus, as that person has to provide corn dough *tamales* for all on the February 2 feast day of Candlemas, which commemorates the presentation of Jesus at the Temple.

independence heroes. As previously described, the coat of arms in the center is inspired by the Aztec legend of the founding of Tenochtitlán by the nomadic Mexica, after the sun god Huitzilopochtli told them to settle where they found an eagle perched on a prickly pear, devouring a snake.

February/March: Carnaval

Carnival is the last big blowout before the privations of Lent, and is celebrated on a grand scale with parties, parades, beauty queens, marching bands, floats, fireworks, and costumed revels. The colorful chaos continues day and night with non-stop dancing and

Carnaval dancer in traditional costume in Huehues.

drinking, and revelers throwing water and *cascarones*—
eggshells filled with confetti. The biggest celebrations are
held in Mazatlán in Sinaloa, Veracruz on the Gulf coast,
Baja California, and Mérida in Yucatán.

March/April: Semana Santa

Holy Week is one of the biggest vacations of the year. It
is in fact a two-week holiday, and Mexicans head off en
masse to beaches and picturesque towns to visit relatives
or to attend the processions, masses, and passion plays that
reenact the crucifixion and resurrection of Jesus Christ in
full gory detail on Jueves Santo (Maundy Thursday) and
Viernes Santo (Good Friday). On Sábado de Gloria (Easter

Children's choir singing in a Good Friday procession in San Miguel de Allende.

Saturday) large papier-mâché effigies representing
unpopular politicians or figures of ridicule are filled
with fireworks and gleefully exploded in the "*quema
de Judas*" (burning of Judas). In many places, such as
Oaxaca and Chiapas, Indigenous and Catholic beliefs
and rituals come together in spectacles of costume,
prayer, and dance. The elaborate Teguinada celebrations
of the Tarahumara (Rarámuri) of Copper Canyon
combine mock battles between horned Pharisees and
Roman soldiers with ancient fertility and rain rituals
that involve the Sun and Moon gods, shamanism,
dancing around the church to the sounds of violin
and drums, and gallons of *tesgüino* (maize beer).

April 25: Feria de San Marcos

This is a huge state fair in Aguascalientes that starts a week before St. Mark's Day and continues for another two weeks. The festival is famous for its cockfights, bullfights, *charreadas* (rodeos), and performances by Mexico's top performers, particularly mariachi stars.

May 5: Cinco de Mayo

Not to be confused with Mexican Independence Day. In Mexico, celebrations mainly take place in Puebla, where

Students commemorate the anniversary of the Battle of Puebla on May 5 in Puebla.

on May 5, 1862, a poorly equipped Mexican force led by General Ignacio Zaragoza defeated an invading French army that was marching on Mexico City from Veracruz.

May 10: Día de la Madre

Mother's Day is a big event, given the importance of the family, with mothers receiving cards, flowers, and even treats at work.

May/June, First Thursday after Trinity Sunday: Corpus Christi

This Catholic feast day celebrates the consecration of the Eucharist as the body and blood of Christ. Processions take place all over the country, and firework towers called *castillos* add to the festive atmosphere. A popular tradition in Puebla is to buy *mulitas* (little models of mules) and to dress children in Indigenous costumes. In Papantla, in Veracruz state, death-defying *voladores* (flyers) continue a pre-Columbian tradition linked to fertility rituals and sun worship. Groups of five men climb a high pole and while one sits at the top and plays a flute, the other four spin around the pole attached only by a rope tied around their waists. The *voladores* descend gradually as they circle the pole, each flyer making thirteen revolutions for a total of fifty-two, representing the 52-year cycle of the Mesoamerican calendar.

June 1: Día de la Marina

Navy Day is celebrated with military parades in port towns.

July, last two Mondays: Guelaguetza

A major folk and handicrafts festival, Guelaguetza takes place in Oaxaca and harks back to a pre-Columbian maize festival dedicated to the goddess Centeotl.

A riot of color, it features regional folk dances, the election of a "goddess" rather than a beauty queen, and a reenactment of the life of the last Zapotec princess, Donají.

Girls dressed in traditional clothes take part in a procession during Guelaguetza in Oaxaca.

September 16: Independence Day

Independence Day is a national holiday with parades, fireworks, and traditional music in celebration of the "Grito de Dolores" (Cry of Dolores), Padre Miguel Hidalgo's call for Mexican independence from Spain in 1810. In a televised address from the balcony of the Palacio Nacional at 11:00 p.m. every September 15, the president of the day reenacts the Grito in front of a huge crowd in Mexico City's main square, the *Zócalo*, by unfurling the Mexican flag, ringing the Dolores bell, and calling out the names of independence heroes: "*Viva Hidalgo! Viva Morelos! Viva Josefa Ortiz de Domínguez! Viva Allende! Vivan Aldama y Matamoros! Viva la independencia nacional! Viva México! Viva México! Viva México!*"

October 12: Día de la Raza

To mark the fateful arrival of Christopher Columbus in the Americas in 1492, the Día de la Raza (Day of the Race) was seen as a celebration of the *mestizaje* that led to the birth of modern Mexico. More recently, in many places it is marked as the Día de la Resistencia Indígena (Day of Indigenous Resistance), a moment to reflect on the Mexican civilizations here before the Spanish conquest, such as the Olmecs, Maya, and Aztecs.

October: Festival Internacional Cervantino

This, the biggest arts festival in Mexico, takes place in Guanajuato in central Mexico. Theater groups, dance troupes, and musicians come from around the world to perform.

October 31–November 2: Día de Muertos (Hanal Pixan in the Yucatán)

The Day of the Dead is Mexico's most defining festival and despite its name is no somber occasion, but rather a vibrant affirmation of life. The belief is that departed loved ones have divine permission to visit friends and relatives once a year, and they are welcomed in homes and in local cemeteries decorated with *altares* (altars) filled with *ofrendas* (offerings) of food and drinks for the spirits to enjoy, and candles, incense, sugar skulls, and bright orange and yellow *cempasuchil* (marigold) flowers to guide

Participants at the Day of the Dead parade in Mexico City.

them. The festival begins on October 31 with the Día de los Angelitos (Day of the Little Angels) dedicated to children and finishes on November 2. In the Yucatán the festival incorporates local food and Mayan elements and is called Hanal Pixan, which means "food for the souls." Before James Bond battled his way through crowds of skeleton-masked Mexicans in the opening credits of the film *Spectre*, there was no Day of the Dead Parade in Mexico City. Seeing the tourism potential, the local CDMX government has since created an annual parade, the Desfile de Día de Muertos, which is now one of the greatest spectacles in the country. Since 2022, the Zócalo, the city's main square, has been filled with all manner of skeletal characters and mega-*ofrendas* in the lead-up to the celebrations. In 2008, Día de Muertos was added to UNESCO's Intangible Cultural Heritage of Humanity list.

December 12: Día de la Virgen de Guadalupe

The Feast of the Virgin of Guadalupe brings tens of thousands of pilgrims from all over the world to worship at the Basílica de Nuestra Señora de Guadalupe. Some come in Indigenous dress, others in simple smocks, and many inch their way on their knees, rosaries in hand, to show their devotion. A modern circular church built in 1974 houses the original image of the dark-haired, brown-skinned Virgin Mary that miraculously appeared on the *tilma* (tunic) of an Aztec convert to Catholicism called Juan Diego in 1531 (see page 79). The image of the Virgin of Guadalupe is without doubt the holiest relic in Mexico and all of Latin America, inspiring both the devotion and the fervent patriotism of the Mexican people. So many pilgrims come to see the revered image that the basilica has been fitted with a series of moving walkways: conveyor belts to speed the faithful along as they snap away on their smartphones.

While pilgrims visit the old basilica with its subsiding, wonky walls, and the chapel on the hill where the second apparition took place, dancers and musicians dressed in Aztec garb called *concheros* bring a splash of pre-Columbian spectacle to the huge plaza.

December 16–24: Posadas

These are candlelit family and church processions that mark the start of Christmas with a reenactment of the story of Joseph and Mary, who arrived in Bethlehem and had to knock on doors to find a *posada* (guesthouse). People sing *villancicos* (Christmas carols) as they go from house to house in the neighborhood, and processions traditionally culminate with a *piñata*, a papier-mâché figure filled with sweets and hung from a rope. Children are blindfolded and take turns to bash at the *piñata* with a stick until it breaks and the sweets are released.

December 24 and 25: Navidad

Christmas is a time when Mexican families gather to eat together, share presents, and set off some fireworks. Noche Buena (Christmas Eve) is the main celebration, with many families attending a mass in the church—including a late *misa de gallo* (midnight mass)—and singing *villancicos*. Christmas dinner is eaten late, and varies around the country from traditional *bacalao*

Breaking a *piñata* at a traditional Navidad *posada* party.

(salted cod) and *guajolote* (turkey) to *lechón* (suckling pig). Other dishes include *tamales* and an Aztec dish called *romeritos,* a stringy rosemary-like herb that is cooked like spinach and served in a *mole* sauce with shrimp patties. Drinks include wine, beer, cider, and *ponche*, a hot fruit punch with cinnamon. Presents are generally given on Christmas Eve, although, as mentioned above, many children still receive their main presents on January 6. Christmas Day is spent visiting family, relaxing, and eating *recalentado*—reheated leftovers from the big blowout the day before.

December 28: Día de los Santos Inocentes

The Day of the Holy Innocents is so-called because of the biblical story of King Herod ordering the massacre of children under two years in Bethlehem in a vain attempt to kill the baby Jesus. Now it's a day to prey on the innocent and gullible with jokes and pranks, like April Fool's Day in the US and the UK.

> ### *Happy Saint's Day*
> There's a saint in the Catholic calendar for every day of the year, and in the past people were named after the *santo* (saint) whose feast day they were born on. Nowadays, names are more loosely tied to the Church, but people still receive cards, small gifts, or just a phone call from their family to wish them well on their saint's day, as if it were a second birthday.

SAINTS' DAYS AND PILGRIMAGES

Towns and villages around Mexico will generally have at least one celebration to honor the patron saint of their church. Saints' days are also celebrated with pilgrimages to their shrines. San Antonio Abad is the patron saint of animals. On his feast day, January 17, people come to churches with dogs, cats, sheep, calves, hamsters, goldfish, even iguanas, so the priests can sprinkle holy water on the pets. In Taxco, Guerrero State, the church service culminates with a contest for the animal with the best costume. The most important pilgrimage in Mexico culminates on December 12 at the Basilica of Our Lady of Guadalupe, the patron saint of Mexico.

MIRACULOUS MANIFESTATION OF OUR LADY OF GUADALUPE

The spiritual heart of Mexico, and the country's most important pilgrimage site, is the shrine to Nuestra Señora de Guadalupe (Our Lady of Guadalupe), an enormous modern basilica on the outskirts of Mexico City. The main focus of devotion is a venerated image of the Virgin Mary that miraculously appeared on the *tilma* (agave-fiber cloak) of a Nahua-speaking native called Juan Diego de Cuautitlán on December 9, 1531.

As the story goes, the Holy Mother appeared to Juan Diego as he was passing the hill of Tepeyac, which coincidentally housed a shrine to the Aztec mother goddess Tonantzin. To calm the astonished Aztec after appearing before him in a burst of radiant light, the Virgin Mary reportedly said: "Do not be afraid. Am I not here, I who am your mother?" She then told Juan Diego to instruct the local bishop to build a church on the site in her honor, but the bishop ignored him. The Virgin then appeared again on December 12, telling Juan Diego to pick flowers from the hill and take them to the bishop. When the astonished bishop saw the beautiful flowers and an image of the Virgin imprinted on the *tilma* he was convinced that Juan Diego's story was true and the first shrine to Our Lady of Guadalupe was built in 1533.

Some have cast doubt on the miracle, suggesting the story of Juan Diego and the radiant Virgin was just a myth cooked up by the Catholic clergy to speed up the conversion of the Indigenous population. They point out that the name Guadalupe comes from the Virgin of Guadalupe in Extremadura, Spain, the place where Hernán Cortés and many of his fellow conquistadors were born. Despite the naysayers, Juan Diego became the first Indigenous saint from the Americas when he was beatified by Pope John Paul II in 2002, and the Basilica of Our Lady of Guadalupe continues to be the most visited Catholic shrine on the planet.

Basilica of Our Lady of Guadalupe in Mexico City.

"WITCHCRAFT" AND SUPERSTITION

Many superstitions are found in Mexico, a legacy of the country's melting pot of cultural traditions. Some superstitions came with the Spanish from Europe; some from the Catholic Church; others derive from the beliefs and rituals of Mexico's pre-Columbian past and surviving Indigenous groups.

Mexicans share the belief that black cats bring bad luck, and that thirteen is an unlucky number—although the day to dread is *martes* 13 (Tuesday 13), not Friday 13. In keeping with Catholic tradition, rather than cross their fingers, people will typically make the sign of the cross when they want to positively influence the outcome of an event or stave off some impending disaster.

Brujería (witchcraft) is an important element of daily life in Mexico and far from the Western stereotype of old crones on broomsticks. Walk into any market in Mexico and you'll find stalls selling herbs, candles, and perfumes guaranteed to bring you love and success, and others to counteract the *envidia* (envy) of others.

There is a widespread belief, especially in rural and Indigenous communities, in *mal de ojo* (the evil eye), a type of curse that can bring bad luck or ill health, especially to children. Amulets of red beads or coral are worn to protect against *mal de ojo,* and children thought to be suffering from its effects are taken to see folk healers and shamans who use incense, tobacco smoke, and incantations to cure them. One home remedy is the *limpia de huevo* (egg cleansing), in which an egg is rubbed all over the child's body and then cracked into a bowl that is left under the child's bed overnight to absorb all the bad energy.

Curanderos (spiritual healers), *brujos* (witches), and shamans practice their arts all over Mexico. Some work in clinics, like doctors, others employ ancient rituals in places of power, such as waterfalls, or at archaeological sites. In Chiapas, the local Tzotzil Maya shamans of San Juan Chamula practice healing rituals that combine Catholic elements with Mayan rituals involving copal incense and a local liquor called *pox* (pronounced "posh") to achieve trance states that allow them to diagnose and cure the spiritual ills affecting the patient's two souls.

In the north of Mexico, the isolation of the Huichol people of the Sierra Madre Mountains has helped to preserve their complex spiritual beliefs and rituals. Their rich symbolism, involving the sun god and his eagle wife, corn, deer, snakes, and fire, is expressed in brightly colored weavings that are highly prized by collectors. The Huichol have a reputation as great healers and employ the hallucinogenic peyote cactus to open the way to the spirit realm.

NARCO SAINTS

Among the many religious statues on sale in markets and street stalls you will come across images of the so-called "Narco Saints," like the Santa Muerte, a skeletal women draped in a long cloak, and Jesús Malverde, a Robin Hood-like folk saint from Sinaloa with a matinée-idol moustache.

Criminals pray to these saints for protection from the authorities and their enemies, while Mexicans who live in areas with high crime rates and migrants who make the difficult journey north to the USA pray to them for protection.

In Culiacán, capital of Sinaloa State, the status of the cult of Jesús Malverde is such that there is a *capilla* (chapel) dedicated to his worship right in the center of the city. The 2021 series about the "generous bandit," as he is sometimes known, called *Malverde: El Santo Patrón* (Malverde: The Patron Saint) proved a popular success and was subsequently signed by Netflix.

Incense sticks for different saints including Jesús Malverde, Protector of the Narcos.

CHAPTER FOUR

MAKING FRIENDS

Mexicans are friendly, gregarious, and enjoy socializing in groups. Families are large and family ties are strong, so most Mexicans have a social circle that centers on the home, the extended family, and neighbors. Non-family friends and workmates may be invited home for birthday parties or to family events like christenings and weddings, but generally people meet up with friends in restaurants and bars, or at a picnic in the park.

Foreigners working in Mexico will find that their Mexican colleagues are quick to invite them for an after-work drink or a meal out, which is a good first step for making friends.

An invitation home to meet the family is quite a big deal. If you turn it down you could offend. Make sure to take a gift, like a decent bottle of tequila or wine, and keep in mind that all attempts you make to speak Spanish, try new foods, join in with the dancing, and generally have fun will be greatly appreciated. Stand on ceremony, or stubbornly refuse to join in the limbo dancing, and you risk being labeled an *aguafiestas* (killjoy, or party pooper)!

Three generations cooking together at home in Mexico City.

THE LANGUAGE BARRIER

One of the biggest problems facing newcomers in Mexico is the language barrier. A lack of conversational Spanish can sap your spontaneity and smother your style. A night out may feel stilted when you are limited to set phrases, frantic miming, or resorting to translation apps. Ever hospitable, Mexicans will still include you in social events and try to explain expressions and jokes, but the bottom line is that it's harder to click with people when you don't have the lingo. Spanish classes will not only give you confidence, new vocabulary, and feedback on your delivery, but also provide a place to make friends with fellow newcomers and a teacher who can fill you in on local culture, new places to eat, and popular hangouts.

Mexico City has plenty of language schools for learning Spanish, but for a more laid-back immersion head to colonial Guanajuato, foodie-favorite Oaxaca, the popular holiday resort of Puerto Vallarta, or the arty, expat-favored San Miguel de Allende.

WHAT'S IN A NAME

A lot of Mexican humor is based on witty wordplay and *double entendre*, and Mexicans enjoy getting playful with people's names. First there are the short forms: Francisco becomes Pancho or Paco, Guillermo is shortened to Memo, Eduardo to Lalo, Jesús to Chucho or Chuy, José to Chepe, Guadalupe to Lupe or Lupita, Concepción to Conchita, and María del Refugio for some reason is shortened to Cuca.

If that isn't confusing enough, almost everybody in Mexico has an *apodo* (nickname), usually given to them at school and generally with the intention of poking fun at them. Sometimes the names are ironic, so the skinniest guy in the group will be called "El Gordo" (Fatty) and the best-looking "El Feo" (Ugly). But usually nicknames are literal and can sometimes sound politically incorrect to Western ears, especially when the fairest girl in the group is called "La Güerita" (Little Blondie), the one with Amerindian features "La Chinita" (Little Chinese Girl), the darkest girl "La Negrita" (Little Black Girl), and the slimmest "La Calaca" (Skeleton).

And then there are Mexico's most famous drug lords. As anybody who has binged the Netflix series Narcos: Mexico will know, the diminutive Joaquín Guzmán is known to the world as "El Chapo" ("Shorty," from *chaparro*), the fearsome Óscar Guerrero was rather bizarrely called "El Winnie Pooh," and Amado Carrillo Fuentes had the grand moniker of "El Señor de los Cielos" (The Lord of the Skies).

Long-term visitors sometimes complain that it's hard to meet people in Mexico, and that they have few acquaintances in their building or neighborhood. If you find yourself in this position, do what the Mexicans do and make a point of saying "*Buenos días!*" or "*Buenas tardes!*" to your neighbors, the guy in the newspaper kiosk, and the girl on the juice stand. Introduce yourself, ask people their names, and remember them for next time. Before you know it, you'll be up to speed on the gossip about local characters and might even get a nickname of your own, like El Gringo Loco (The Mad Gringo).

FASHIONABLY LATE

When it comes to social engagements, British punctuality will not win you any friends. Turn up to a party on the dot, and you are likely to find the Mexican girl who invited you is still doing her hair and is not amused at having to entertain you while she finishes getting dressed. Whatever the occasion—even weddings, christenings, and funerals—people tend to turn up at least half an hour late. This tardiness is such a fact of life that if you really want people to turn up at 8:00 p.m. you invite them for 7:30. Even so, you should still expect some of your guests to show up after 9:00. Equally, if you're waiting for a date to arrive, wait at least twenty minutes past the arranged time before sending a terse text. The secret is to go with the flow and relax into a more Mexican concept of time.

CONVERSATION STARTERS AND STOPPERS

Mexicans like to keep things light-hearted when socializing and will seek common ground, asking you about your family, your favorite music, food, beer, and what you think about Mexico. Needless to say, this is not an invitation to launch into a list of the things you think are wrong with the country. People in Mexico are very proud of their country and are sensitive to criticism of it, especially given its difficult history with the US. While locals might gripe about the pollution levels in Mexico

City, the surreal absurdity of the latest political scandal, or the tragic human toll of the war on drugs, a foreign visitor doing the same isn't likely to be appreciated. Of course, as your relationships with locals become more established, it will be increasingly acceptable to engage in more candid conversation about life in Mexico.

THE DATING GAME

If navigating the language can be tricky in a foreign land, trying to find love (*buscando amor)*, with all the cultural nuances involved, can be a minefield. In Mexico, the love game is still quite traditional, with men expected to treat the objects of their passion with effusive declarations of undying love, gifts of flowers and chocolates, and unexpected mariachi serenades.

This old-school attitude is reflected in the general courtesies and gallantry shown to women: opening doors for them, paying for everything on a night out, and making sure they are delivered safely to their door at the end of proceedings. The downside to all this romance can be manifested in soap-opera sensitivities, possessiveness, jealousy, and a difficulty in accepting rejection (as the mariachis illustrate).

In big towns and cities, younger Mexicans are increasingly looking for love via their smartphones, with Tinder being the most popular dating app locally, followed by Bumble. Websites can also be an effective way to meet prospective romantic partners, but steer clear of those that specifically want to hook up locals

A couple share a kiss in Guanajuato.

with foreigners, as some people's motives might be purely financial.

The best way to *ligar* (hook up) is probably to follow the same advice for finding friends. Mexicans are always happy to matchmake, and if you build up a group of friends from work, expat connections, or networking sites, they will soon start introducing you to possible soul mates. This can work well, as going out in a group takes the pressure out of that first date, and will expand your social circle.

EXPAT FRIENDLY

Mexico came top out of sixty-one countries in a 2022 survey carried out by InterNations, an international networking group, aimed at finding the best (and worst) places for expatriates to settle. Mexico got top marks for ease of settling into the local culture, and in the categories of Culture, Local Friendliness, and Finding Friends.

The overwhelming majority of expats surveyed described locals as friendly, and 75 percent said they were easy to make friends with. Most expats loved the culinary variety and dining options, as well as the natural environment. Although Mexico doesn't rank well for safety and security (it ranked 41st out of 52 countries) overall, the survey found that 91 percent of respondents were happy with their life there.

EXPAT GROUPS

With multinational companies employing thousands of foreign workers in Mexico City, Guadalajara, and Monterrey, and more than

---

1.6 million US citizens resident in the country in 2022, one way to widen your social circle is to join an expat group.

Retirement havens like Ajijic on Lake Chapala and San Miguel de Allende have a full calendar of activities and cultural events in English and Spanish. In the Yucatán, and resort towns like Ensenada, Playas de Rosarito, and Puerto Vallarta, the local expat communities are swollen by "snowbirds" from the USA and Canada in winter months, and you'll have no trouble finding English-language activities to ease you into local living.

The international social networking group InterNations has chapters in Mexico City, Guadalajara, Monterrey, and Puerto Vallarta, and offers young and not-so-young expats the opportunity to meet up with old hands and locals at cocktail evenings, brunch meetings, *taco* tastings, sporting events, and cinema nights. Another international networking site in Mexico is meetup.com, which is a great place to find groups organizing a host of events and activities, from book groups to chess clubs, language exchanges, and Latin dance nights.

Facebook also has large groups focused on specific cities in Mexico where you can turn for advice on everything from where to get your favorite brand of peanut butter to how to fill out visa forms.

CHAPTER FIVE

AT HOME

Mexican homes are as varied as the Mexicans who inhabit them. They range from the luxury penthouses with swimming pools and servants of the urban mega-rich, to the spacious, Spanish-style haciendas of rural landowners. For the middle class there are the gentrified *colonias* (neighborhoods) of two- or three-story houses in the hearts of the cities, apartments in shiny skyscrapers offering the latest "mod cons," or new-build houses in suburbs on the outskirts. A working-class family might rent a high-rise concrete apartment in one of the vast social-housing projects constructed in the 1970s, while the urban poor are crammed into the sprawling *ciudades perdidas* (shanty towns) that encircle the country's major cities. In the Yucatán, the Maya still build distinctive single-story oval houses with adobe walls and thatched roofs that have changed little in centuries.

Aerial view of Mexico City's Paseo de la Reforma.

RISE OF THE CITIES

Since the 1900s there has been a steady movement from the countryside to urban centers. In 1900 only 10 percent of the population lived in cities, but the balance started to shift with the upheavals of the Mexican Revolution in 1910 and later moves to industrialize the economy. Nowadays, some 80 percent of Mexicans live in cities, the majority of them in the country's four main urban centers—Mexico City, Guadalajara, Puebla, and Monterrey—and in the border towns of Juárez and Tijuana.

The main magnet for those looking to improve their lives is still the behemoth that is Mexico City, which has expanded to absorb so many of the surrounding towns and suburbs that the Mexico City Metropolitan Area now has a population of over 22 million people,

making it the largest metropolitan area in the Western Hemisphere, the tenth-largest city on the planet, and the largest Spanish-speaking city in the world. The city also encompasses the Neza-Chalco-Itza shanty town, which with four million inhabitants is considered the largest slum in the world.

MADRE KNOWS BEST

As we've seen, Mexico has a reputation of being a rather "macho" country, but at the heart of the family and the home is generally a mother or grandmother who holds everything together. Although things are slowly changing, women still have responsibility for overseeing the cooking, cleaning, and childcare, and in many cases this is likely to be in addition to holding down a full-time job. Women will also often manage the family budget: paying bills, doing the weekly shopping, and organizing family events such as Christmas, birthdays, and christenings.

As discussed, this matriarchal setup is deeply rooted in Mexican culture and has played a critical role in a country where historically many fathers have had to work away from the family home for long periods. The strong national devotion to Mexico's patron saint, Our Lady of Guadalupe, also known as the Holy Mother, is a reflection of the reverence in which mothers are held.

A word to the wise: "your mother" jokes might be popular among friends in the US but insult a Mexican's mother at your peril.

HOME HELP

From the uniformed maids, nannies, chauffeurs, and gardeners of the mega-rich, to the lady who comes in once a week to clean up and help a working mother with the ironing, many people in Mexico have some sort of home help. Most professionals will have someone who comes and cleans once a week or more, and very often they will run errands, wash clothes, and cook a meal as well.

For the rich and upper-middle class, having servants is seen as a status symbol. Live-in maids are a luxury that many can afford as they are generally paid less than the minimum wage in return for room and board. Some of them will have worked in a family for years, and will have built up a relationship with several generations. Employers might pay for the education of a maid's children and throw them parties on their birthdays.

Employer-employee relationships are not always so benevolent, however, and protests over the protection of domestic workers under labor laws led to the government passing ILO Convention 189 in May 2019, a landmark piece of legislation that granted some 2 million Mexican workers basic rights, including regulated hours of work and paid holidays.

Mexican attitudes to domestic workers may differ from what some foreign visitors are used to, and some adaptation may be necessary. Employing domestic workers is also considered by locals as a way of helping people who would otherwise be underemployed. If you find yourself in need of help at home, there are numerous agencies that specialize in finding domestic workers and will provide references from past employers, but many people rely on recommendations from friends and coworkers.

It's important to be aware that some of the terms used to describe domestic workers are considered derogatory. Many Mexicans will refer to *la empleada* (the hired help), but *la muchacha* or *la 'chacha* (the girl), especially when applied to a mature woman in her forties or fifties, can seem patronizing, and *la sirvienta* (the servant) is inappropriate. Most offensive are *la gata* (the cat) and *la criada* (literally, "raised"), dating back to the time when a family would take in a poor girl as young as ten or twelve to work in their home.

MAID IN MEXICO

Uniformed maids are a mainstay of Mexico's popular telenovelas (soap operas), either as the main characters, or involved in the subplots and intrigues. In the 1960s the rise of maids as protagonists in long-running TV dramas like *Maria Isabel* reflected the growing number of poor young women, many of them from Indigenous cultures, who came to the capital to work in the houses of the wealthy. Afternoon timeslots for the telenovelas were even tweaked so that domestic workers could tune in between cleaning up after lunch and serving dinner.

Many soap operas have reworked the Cinderella tale of a poor servant girl who finds happiness in the arms of the handsome son of a wealthy family, but the reality is rarely so romantic. Mexico's live-in maids work long hours for low pay, often far from their families, and despite the recent introduction of labor laws protecting their rights, they more often than not have no written contract outlining their duties, hours, or salary, leaving them open to exploitation.

Mexican director Alfonso Cuarón's 2018 Oscar-winning Netflix drama *Roma* is an intensely moving ode to the Mixtec maid (Mixtec being one of Mexico's Indigenous groups) who looked after him as a boy in Colonia Roma neighborhood of Mexico City in the 1970s. The maid and main protagonist of the film, Cleodegaria "Cleo" Gutiérrez, is played by Yalitza Aparicio, a Mixtec-Trique primary school teacher from Oaxaca who is also the first Indigenous American woman to receive a Best Actress Oscar nomination. The actress has since used her fame to campaign for the rights of domestic workers and Indigenous women.

DAILY LIFE

Forget the stereotype of a sombrero-wearing Mexican stretched out in the shade, calmly watching the world go by. Daily life for most Mexicans involves a hectic schedule, juggling work and family commitments, a few hours on public transport commuting across town, and a fair dose of socializing once the sun goes down.

Mexico's middle class has grown dramatically over the last twenty years to about 35–40 percent of the population, but another 40 percent still live in poverty, and the gulf between the "haves" and the "have nots," especially in rural areas, continues to pose a problem for Mexican society.

Wherever Mexicans live, food plays an important role and is generally still cooked from scratch. For many wives and mothers, the first task of the day involves cooking corn *tortillas* on a griddle, and making coffee to have with *pan dulce* (sweet rolls). A light *desayuno* (breakfast) at home is usually supplemented by a street snack or *antojito* (literally, "little craving"), such as *gorditas, quesadillas,* or *tacos de*

A woman adding corn to *posole* hominy and pork soup.

nopal (cactus paddle *tacos*). For a more substantial breakfast, maybe at the weekend after a big night out, Mexicans will have *chilaquiles,* made of crunchy fried *tortilla* triangles cooked in a spicy tomato sauce and topped with cheese, or *huevos rancheros*, with a couple of fried eggs on *tortillas* topped with refried beans and a *salsa*. A Yucatán variation called *huevos motuleños* also includes ham, peas, and plantain with spicy *salsa* and corn *tortillas* for a full blowout.

The working day can start as early as 5:00 a.m. for those who have to commute long distances or set up market stalls, and offices generally start work at around 8:00 to 8:30 a.m. By 10:30 or 11:00 a.m. it's time for *almuerzo*—either coffee with *pan dulce* or more *antojitos*.

Lunch, known as *comida* or *comida fuerte* (literally, "heavy meal"), is usually the main meal of the day and is often eaten at *taquerías* (*taco* stands) or small restaurants called *fondas* or *loncherías* that serve set-menu lunches at cheap prices.

In the countryside the day finishes earlier for many

people, but in cities offices close by about 7:00 p.m. and a light *cena* (evening meal) is eaten late, at 8:00–9:00 p.m., either at home with the family, or out at a food stall, bar, or restaurant with friends or workmates. Inviting friends back home to eat with the family is not usual, so if you do get an invitation you can feel quite privileged.

On weekends, after drinks at bars or *cantinas*, the late-night action usually ends up at a *taquería* or street stall serving *antojitos*.

EVERYDAY SHOPPING

In the big cities you can easily find shiny supermarkets and US chains like Walmart and Costco, but most people in Mexico continue to do their food shopping in large covered markets or at local street stalls.

The markets offer a chance to chat with stallholders and try the food before you buy. The colorful piles of chili peppers, vegetables, exotic fruit, and cuts of meat on sale stimulate the senses and offer inspiration to jaded cooks. Markets are also some of the best places to enjoy a fruit juice or a traditional Mexican dish. Sit-down food stalls sell a range of *antojitos, comidas*, and favorites like *posole* (hominy and pork soup), *tlayudas* (a Oaxacan *tortilla* dish sometimes described as "Mexican pizza"), and *chapulines* (fried grasshoppers). Mexicans will organize their week around the shops and markets they visit, often buying particular items on specific days, and picking up whatever's in season or on special offer.

In Mexico City the huge Mercado la Merced has one

of the biggest ranges of market food in the country and is also a good place to pick up mops, brooms, and buckets. Nearby is the sprawling Mercado de Sonora, known by locals as the *mercado de los brujos* (witches' market). People come here for the eclectic selection of medicinal herbs, potions, amulets, religious icons, colored candles, and various strange and spooky items. You can get your palm read, have aromatic incense wafted over you to banish evil spirits, and pick up a perfume that makes you irresistible to the opposite sex. Intriguingly perhaps for a market full of icons of the Santa Muerte, people also come here to buy children's toys, costumes, and *piñata*.

Cholula de Rivadabia Centro Market in Cholula, Puebla.

The University of Guanajuato, main campus.

EDUCATION

Having a good education is highly prized in Mexico. Public schools are free to all from six to fifteen years of age, but standards in the state education sector vary considerably, especially in rural areas, and there is a significant dropout rate.

Another factor affecting public schools is the teachers' union, the Sindicato Nacional de Trabajadores de la Educación (SNTE), which has some 1.4 million members and is one of the most powerful trade unions in Latin America. Corruption charges have dogged union leaders, and protests by teachers and disputes with breakaway unions have slowed the pace of educational reform.

Some parents make huge sacrifices to send their children to private schools to improve their future prospects. These can range from small, one-room schools in rural areas to grand colleges where the kids are dropped off by chauffeurs and nannies. At the top are *colegios bilingües* (bilingual schools), which teach in English as well as Spanish and cater to the children of the elite and expats.

In most towns and cities you will find a profusion of private schools and colleges catering to working adults who return to education in their twenties and thirties. These colleges offer night school classes in English, law, accountancy, hairdressing, and dentistry.

For middle- and upper-class Mexicans, attending a good school, getting a place at a good university, and doing a Master's or MBA abroad are seen as the keys to a good career.

The School System

Compulsory free education in the public school system starts in pre-school, which is compulsory for three- to five-year-olds. Obligatory education extends to *primaria* (primary school) for children aged six to twelve, and *secundaria* (secondary school or junior high), from ages thirteen to fifteen. *Prepa* (short for *preparatoria*) is the equivalent of high school, and prepares students for entry into a university or technical college. This level is not compulsory; the reality is that most young people leave at the end of secondary school, and some before that.

Both public and private schools have to follow the curriculum laid down by the Secretaría de Educación

Pública (the Public Education Ministry) during a regular 8:00 a.m. to 1:00 p.m. school day, but private schools generally offer extra subjects and will often have a longer school day, or after-school classes extending into the afternoon.

LEARNING ENGLISH

Given Mexico's long border with its English-speaking neighbor to the north, the large number of Mexicans crossing the border to work or employed by US firms in Mexico, and the millions of English-speaking tourists who visit each year, it's no surprise that there are many eager students taking English classes in Mexico's numerous language schools. What is a little more surprising perhaps is that so few Mexicans can speak English, considering the compulsory English classes children attend at primary and secondary school.

In border towns, tourist resorts, and major cities it's not too hard to find somebody with some command of English, but this is less likely in rural areas and even rarer in Indigenous communities where Spanish is a second language.

One advantage of this interest in English for the visitor is that many people will want to practice their English-language skills on you, and will hopefully reciprocate by teaching you a few words or phrases in Spanish.

THE CYCLE OF FAMILY LIFE AND RITES OF PASSAGE

For both rich and poor the cycle of family life—births, baptisms, weddings, birthdays, and *quinceañera*

parties—brings family and friends together. If you spend any time traveling in Mexico, or have a job working alongside Mexicans, you might well be lucky enough to receive an invitation to one of these events. If you do, accepting the invitation is highly recommended and will provide you with real insight into Mexican life.

A young girl at her First Communion.

Milestones Marked by the Catholic Church

El bautizo (baptism), when a child receives his or her Christian name, is usually celebrated shortly after birth at a church service attended by family and close friends. This is a joyous occasion where gifts are given, and there is typically a post-baptism party with music, food, and drink.

Primera Comunión (First Communion) is when young Catholics between the ages of seven and twelve first take the consecrated wafer and wine that symbolize the body and blood of Christ. Typically celebrated in a group, boys and girls dress all in white, with white gloves and a white candle symbolizing purity. Boys often wear long-sleeved *guayabera* shirts and girls wear veils or floral headbands.

Confirmación (Confirmation) takes place at around fifteen or sixteen years old, when young adults confirm their Catholic faith in the church at a special mass.

Sweet Fifteen

A major event for young Mexican girls is the *Fiesta de Quince Años* (Fifteenth Birthday Party), which is seen as a rite of passage into womanhood. The elaborate celebrations are more like a wedding than a Sweet Sixteen party in the US. Depending on the budget, the fifteen-year-old *quinceañera* dresses up in a ball gown with a crown or tiara and is joined by her closest friends who will also wear formal suits and dresses. Traditionally, a *quince* starts with Mass in church; then there are

Decorations for a *quince* party.

photographs on the church steps; and afterwards there's
the party. The *quinceañera* dances a waltz with her father,
followed by a toast, perhaps a serenade by a mariachi
band, and then a live band or DJ will play into the night.
Quinceañera presents can be extravagant. At one time,
a trip to the US was all the rage for the daughters of the
rich; nowadays presents can include tours around Europe,
and even a car. For poorer families the dress might be
homemade, and the party held at home, but everybody
tries to make the day special for the *quinceañera*.

Weddings

There are few festive occasions in Mexico as joyous,
colorful, or costly as a wedding. By law you are not
married until you have had a civil wedding, so couples
who want to marry in a church will have a civil wedding
first. The easiest and cheapest option is to get married at
a *registro civil* (register office), but if you can afford it, a
Justice of the Peace will come and marry you at home,
in a historic *hacienda*, or on the beach.

For foreigners wanting to marry other foreigners in
Mexico, the requirements are quite straightforward, and
Cancún and Cozumel have become popular destinations
for beach weddings, especially among Canadians.

Foreigners wanting to marry Mexicans in Mexico
must apply for a special permit known as a Permiso para
Contraer Matrimonio con un Nacional in the federal
state in which they plan to tie the knot.

Traditional church weddings in Mexico can be lavish
affairs, like something out of a telenovela. Traditions
include the *lasso*, or wedding cord, which is a rosary

A typical regional wedding parade, known as Calenda de Bodas, in Oaxaca.

symbolizing eternal unity placed in a figure of eight around the couple or their wrists, and the *arras,* thirteen gold or silver coins given by the groom to the bride. Mayan weddings can include a blessing by a shaman with copal incense.

Wedding receptions are lively, with mariachi bands, tequila, and traditional food. One colorful tradition is the *baile de billete*, in which guests pin bills to the bride and groom as they dance around the room. Another tradition is *el muertito* ("the little corpse"), where the band plays the funeral march to signify that the groom's days of partying are over, and he is thrown up into the air by the male guests. In Veracruz, a Huastec tradition is to serve guests a huge stuffed *tamale* called a *zacahuil*.

CHAPTER SIX

TIME OUT

Mexicans work hard. Long working hours are the norm, and more so for those in rural areas. It's no surprise then that Mexicans value their free time and, in general, enjoy spending it as they do their fiestas: with family and friends, and preferably with food, drinks, and music. The annual calendar of folk festivals and public holidays offers plenty of opportunities for carousing, and on weekends people gather in groups at local parks to play sports, enjoy a picnic, or just laugh off their troubles and down a few *chelitas* (beers). The more adventurous head off to the country's many beaches, archaeological sites, or *pueblos magicos* (picturesque towns) to soak up the atmosphere, chow down on local specialties, and share quality time with loved ones. Museums and cultural institutions are also popular weekend destinations, especially in the big cities.

Whatever the destination or activity, food will play a part. Despite the arrival of US fast-food chains, Mexicans are natural foodies at heart and eating out revolves around a devotion to authentic Mexican flavors and ancient recipes. People are fiercely proud of their culinary and musical traditions, which have been recognized by UNESCO as unique cultural expressions that must be preserved for future generations.

A vibrant arts scene includes internationally recognized painters and poets, a hugely diverse music scene, world-class museums and galleries, colorful folk arts, and a film industry that continues to produce award-winning movies and that launches the careers of actors, directors, and cinematographers.

When it comes to spectator sports, football is king, followed by baseball and boxing. There are also homegrown sports such as *charreria* (rodeo), the country's official national sport, and *lucha libre* (freestyle wrestling), with larger-than-life *luchadores* donning masks, capes, and tights to delight their baying fans.

MEXICAN FOOD

For a real taste of Mexico, you need only follow the crowds to a bustling street market where the dining experience can be as gastronomically and experientially rewarding as dining in one of Mexico's fancier restaurants, where top chefs reinvent and push the limits on old favorites in novel and exciting ways. The variety of dishes and ingredients on offer around the country is truly remarkable, and you would need years to try all of the country's regional dishes.

Many people arrive with a misconception of Mexican food based on the Tex-Mex concoctions popular in the US and Europe, such as *burritos* (wheat *tortilla* wraps) or hard-shell *tacos* stuffed with shredded meat, refried

Tacos filled with shredded pork.

Tamales, a dough usually made from corn steamed in banana leaves.

beans, guacamole, and thick cream. It may also come
as a surprise to hear that *chili con carne* is not Mexico's
national dish!

Most dishes include *tortilla*, a circular flat bread usually
made from corn dough, although wheat *tortillas* are

popular in northern Mexico. Served piping hot from the griddle, *tortillas* are used to mop up food in place of a fork or spoon.

The First Fusion Food

Mexican cuisine has been called the first fusion food, born from the collision of New World and Old World ingredients and the novel combinations that ensued. Some 8,000 years before Hernán Cortés arrived in Veracruz in 1519, the pre-Hispanic inhabitants of present-day Mexico were eating a diet based on the cultivation of corn, beans, and squash, sometimes referred to as the "three sisters" because they grow so well together and complement each other nutritionally.

Corn was considered a sacred food by the Aztecs and the Mayans. It was the staff of life, ground to a paste on a *metate* (a rough stone grinding slab) to make the dough for *tortillas* cooked on a *comal* (clay griddle), or made into *tamales*, balls of corn dough stuffed with other ingredients and steamed in a corn husk.

The Aztecs harvested *nopales* (cactus paddles) and *tunas* (prickly pears), and they fermented the sap of the maguey or agave plant to make a mildly alcoholic drink called *pulque*. In Lake Texcoco they harvested green algae called *tecuitlatl* (spirulina), which they formed into cakes and ate like cheese. Meat came from *guajolote* (turkey), *pato* (duck), *venado* (deer), and *conejo* (rabbit), but played only a small part in a diet in which most of the protein came from beans, or insects such as *chapulines* (grasshoppers), *chinicuiles* (maguey worms), *escamoles* (ant eggs), and *ahuatle* (water-fly eggs). Pre-Hispanic people also ate *huitlacoche* (also known as *cuitlacoche)*, a fungus that grows on corn, and *jicama*, a thick, crunchy root vegetable.

Many of the ingredients we take for granted today first came to Europe from Mexico, such as tomatoes, avocados, chilies, pineapples, vanilla, and cacao, which the Aztecs made into a foamy chocolate drink with chilies. To Mexico the Spanish brought spices from the East, citrus fruits like oranges and limes, sugarcane, apples, grapes, onions, garlic, rice, wheat, milk, cheese, chicken, pork, lamb, beef, and herbs, such as coriander.

The overall result is a cuisine that is unique, complex, and sophisticated, and in 2010 UNESCO recognized it as an Intangible Cultural Heritage of Humanity.

Little Cravings

Antojitos ("little cravings") are essentially snacks, the sort of finger food served up at *tianguis* (street markets) and small restaurants. The ultimate *antojito* is a *taco*—simply a small *tortilla* with a meat or vegetarian filling or topping. *Tacos* have been called "the most democratic of Mexican foods" because everybody, from the lowliest laborers to the richest mega-moguls, eats them.

Popular fillings at *taquerias* (*taco* stands) include *carnitas* (marinated pork), *campechano* (beef and chorizo sausage), *chicharrón* (pork rinds), *arrachera* (skirt steak), *picadillo* (ground beef), *birria* (goat), *guisado* (chicken or beef stew), *cabeza de res* (the meat from a boiled cow head), *rajas* (roasted *poblano* peppers cut into strips), *nopales* (thin slices of cactus paddle), and *huitlacoche* (Mexican truffle).

In Baja California and on the Pacific coast they make *tacos* with fish and seafood. In Oaxaca you can try them with *escamoles* (ant eggs). Popular in Mexico City are *tacos al pastor,* a variation on the Middle Eastern *shawarma* brought to Mexico by Lebanese immigrants. Marinated pork is skewered on a vertical metal spike to form a *trompo* and cooked as it rotates. The meat is shaved off and served with a slice of pineapple from the top of the *trompo*.

What makes *antojitos* so addictive are the fresh dressings and zingy *salsas* (sauces) you pile on top. Typical accompaniments are a squeeze of lime or lemon, *cebolla* (chopped onions), *cilantro* (coriander), *pico de gallo* (chopped tomato and onion, literally "chicken beak"), *guacamole* (mashed avocado), *salsa verde* (green sauce made from *tomatillo* and chilies), *salsa roja* (red sauce made from fresh tomatoes and chilies), *salsa de chipotle* (a smoky sauce made with *chipotle* peppers), and fiery chilies like *habaneros* and *jalapeños* for those daring enough to try.

A GLOSSARY OF STREET FOOD

Elote: Corn on the cob cooked on the grill, smothered with butter or mayo, rolled in chili powder and cheese, and served on a stick.
Esquites: Shucked corn cooked up in a pot with mild chilies and salt, served in a cup with crumbly cheese and a squeeze of lime.
Flautas: *Tortillas* rolled into flutes and deep-fried.

Enchiladas are similar but must be bathed in a *salsa*. *Enfrijoladas* are bathed in a creamy bean sauce.

Huaraches: Thick, oval *tortillas* in the shape of a *huarache* (sandal), covered with beans, cheese, and a meat or mushroom topping.

Quesadillas: Folded *tortillas* filled with string cheese, mushroom, chorizo, and potato, or *chapulines* (grasshoppers).

Sopes: Small, circular corn dough shells, filled with refried beans, cheese, and a meat or vegetable filling, and topped with fresh chopped tomato or lettuce.

Tamales: Corn dough stuffed with pork, chicken, *salsa verde*, or *mole*, steamed or boiled in a corn husk. In Oaxaca, Chiapas, and the Yucatán they wrap *tamales* in a banana leaf.

Tlacayos: Oval *tortillas* usually made from blue corn, stuffed with beans, and topped with cheese, onions, *nopales*, or *requesón* (*ricotta*).

Tlayudas: Baked *tortillas* topped with refried beans, shredded beef, Oaxacan cheese, and other ingredients. Also known as "Mexican pizza."

Tosta: A bun cut in half and stuffed to bursting with meat, or any other ingredient. In Jalisco, a *tosta ahogado* (drowned) is drenched in a spicy red *salsa*.

Tostadas: Fried *tortillas* topped with refried beans and any of the usual *taco* toppings.

Fresh From the Sea

Mexico has nearly 6,000 miles (9.6 km) of coastline, and the waters of the Pacific, the Gulf, and the Caribbean provide an abundance of *pescado* (fish), including *atún* (tuna), *huachinango* (red snapper), *jurel* (jackfish), and *mero* (grouper). At the beach, fish is usually grilled whole or in fillets, with salt, lemon, and garlic, and served with rice, avocado slices, and *ensalada de col* (cabbage slaw). *Mariscos* (shellfish) include *camarones* (shrimp), *pulpo* (octopus), *calamares* (squid), *langosta* (lobster), *cangrejos* (crab), *callos* (scallops), and *ostiones* (oysters).

The freshest seafood is to be found at beach resorts, but most big towns and cities in the interior will have a *marisquería* (seafood restaurant) or *coctelería* (serving seafood cocktails like *ceviche*). Mexico City, Monterrey, and Guadalajara have some very high-end restaurants serving sophisticated seafood dishes.

Seafood is particularly popular during Quaresma (Lent) and Semana Santa (Easter), when Catholics refrain from eating meat. On Christmas Eve it is traditional to eat *bacalao* (salt cod) with a sauce of tomatoes, olives, chilies, and capers.

The signature dish of Veracruz is *huachinango a la veracruzana*—red snapper cooked in a tomato sauce with olives and *jalapeños*. Another Veracruz specialty, considered a surefire hangover cure and powerful aphrodisiac, is *Vuelve a la Vida* ("return to life"), a *caldo* (broth) of squid, octopus, crab, and whatever else is in season. In some places it is served as a seafood cocktail, made *ceviche*-style with lime, onion, and chilies.

REGIONAL DISHES

Chiles en nogada: Cooked up in 1821 by nuns in Puebla to honor independence hero General Augustín de Iturbide, this delicious Independence Day dish patriotically combines the colors of the Mexican flag. Green *poblano* chilies stuffed with *picadillo* (ground beef) are bathed in a white sauce made from *nueces de nogal* (walnuts) and sprinkled with red pomegranate seeds.

Mole: Pronounced *moh-lay*, this ground mixture of chilies, nuts, and dark chocolate is used to make a thick sauce that is poured over chicken or turkey. *Mole Poblano*, from Puebla, is considered Mexico's national dish, but Oaxaca has seven *mole* recipes of its own, combining local herbs like *hoja santa* with almonds, dried fruits, nuts, and chili varieties like *arbol*, *ancho*, *pasillo*, and *guajillo*. *Manchamantel* ("tablecloth stainer") is a *mole* made with pineapple and spicy chorizo.

Cochinita Pibil: Pork rubbed with *achiote* (annatto paste), marinated in orange juice, wrapped in banana leaves, and cooked in a *pib* (Mayan earth oven). This is the signature dish of the Yucatán, where *recados* (sauces) feature bitter orange for a sweet and sour flavor.

Posole (pozole): A stew of hominy and pork with a garnish of chopped cabbage, radish, and avocado slices from the states of Sinaloa, Michoacán, Guerrero, Zacatecas, Jalisco, Morelos, and CDMX.

Mexican *ceviches* differ slightly from the Peruvian versions, as the fish or seafood is usually diced and served on a *tostada* (fried *tortilla*) with slices of avocado.

Aguachiles—popular in coastal areas of Sinaloa, Nayarit, and Baja California—are similar to *ceviches*, but the shrimps are cured in citrus and a blended mixture of *chiltepín* chili peppers, onions, cilantro and sometimes fruit for a fresh, zesty flavour.

Vegetarians and Vegans

There are plenty of fresh fruits and vegetables to be found in Mexico. At food stalls in markets you can easily put together an order of traditional *tacos*, *gorditas*, *quesadillas*, or simple corn *tortillas* with cheese, bean, or *nopal* (cactus paddle) toppings. These are easily turned into mini-meals with the addition of the fresh garnishes that accompany most dishes. It's also possible to find vegetarian and vegan restaurants in the big cities, at chic resorts that cater to an international crowd, and at some beach hostels catering to backpackers.

With all of the above in mind, there is little widespread understanding in Mexico of what it means to be vegetarian, and so you should take care when ordering food. For example, asking if a dish is *sin carne* only means "without red meat," and not "without meat," so chicken, for example, may be present.

Also, bear in mind that vegetable soups are often made with meat stock, beans are often cooked with chunks of pork, and many dishes are fried in *manteca* (pork lard). When a friend explained to a waiter in Guadalajara "*Soy vegano*" (I'm a vegan), the response was a bemused "*Eso es como un martiano?*" (Is that like a Martian?).

Desserts

Traditional desserts include *flan* (crème caramel), *pastel de tres leches* (three-milk cake), and *pastel de elote* (corn cake). Fruits cooked in *almibar* (syrup) like *ciricote* (geiger fruit) are often served with cheese to offset the sweetness, and tropical fruit combos of mango, papaya, and guava are also popular desserts.

Delicious ice creams, called *nieves* ("snows"), range from creamy concoctions of chocolate, coconut, and condensed milk to fruit sorbets. *Raspados* are snow cones made on the street from shaved ice and flavored syrups, and *paletas* are homemade popsicles.

DRINKS

Juices made with water, sugar, and ice are called *aguas frescas* (fresh waters). Flavors include *tamarindo* (tamarind), *piña* (pineapple), *jamaica* (hibiscus flowers), *betabel* (beetroot), and *horchata* (rice and cinnamon). If you're concerned that unfiltered water was used in the preparation of *aguas frescas* in street markets, opt for freshly squeezed *jugos* (juices). *Licuados* are shakes made with milk, ice, and sugar. *Refrescos* (soft drinks) include all the usual US sodas as well as local brands like Jarritos and Mundet with flavors like *guayaba* (guava) and *manzana* (apple).

For a java kick to get you started, good-quality coffee is widely available, but it's also worth trying *café de olla* ("pot coffee"), a combination of coffee, cinnamon, and sugar traditionally prepared in a clay pot. Herbal teas like *manzanilla* (chamomile) are readily available, but English-style teas are harder to find. For a flavor of the pre-Hispanic past try *atole,* a hot, creamy, cornmeal drink sweetened with *piloncillo* (raw sugar). *Champurrado* is *atole* with chocolate.

A Taxing Solution to Sugary Sodas

Despite the country's rich culinary traditions, its enviable variety of exotic fruit juices, and markets overflowing with fresh produce, Mexicans are among the highest consumers of *refrescos* (soft drinks) in the world per capita, particularly American sodas like Coca Cola. Combined with an unhealthy diet of *comida chatarra* (junk food), this has led to an obesity epidemic and a spike in related health conditions such as diabetes.

In 2014, the Mexican government moved to tackle obesity by implementing a 10 percent tax on sugar-sweetened beverages. Initial studies showed a 12 percent fall in sales of sodas in the first year the tax was applied, but a study in 2020 found that Mexicans were drinking on average no less than 163 liters of soda every year, more than any other nation.

Alcohol

While tequila and *mezcal* (mescal) are Mexico's most famous spirits (see page 126), the country also produces a large selection of good quality beers. *Cerveza* is the

Spanish word for beer, but you're more likely to hear Mexicans ordering *una chela* or *una fría*. "*Vamos a echarnos unas chelitas*" is a slang way of saying, "Let's have some beers."

Two brewing giants dominate the local market. Grupo Modelo, which is owned by the Belgian brewing giant Anheuser-Busch InBev, makes Corona, Negra Modelo, Modelo Especial, León, Victoria, and Pacifico. Its rival Cervecería Cuauhtémoc Moctezuma is a subsidiary of Dutch brewer Heineken and makes Sol, Dos Equis, Tecate, Indio, Bohemia, Carta Blanca, and Superior. The bigger bottles of beer on sale have their own names: a *caguama* ("turtle") or *ballena* ("whale") is any bottle containing 900 ml to a liter. The larger *caguamón or ballenón* contains 1.2 liters.

Cheladas and *micheladas* are lime juice shandies spiced up with worcestershire sauce, tomato juice, or *clamato* (clam broth and tomato juice). They are typically served in an ice-cold pint glass with salt and chili around the rim, or sticky sweet and sour sauces like *chamoy*. *Pulque*, a creamy, viscous "beer" made from the fermented juice of the agave (or maguey) plant, was a sacred drink in Aztec times and until the 1950s the preferred drink of the poor, the working classes, and bohemians. Nowadays, beer rules supreme and it's much harder to find *pulquerías* (*pulque* bars), where *blanco* (straight *pulque*) is sold alongside colorful *curados* (*pulque* flavored with fruit juices, coconut, and wheat). In Mexico City historic *pulquerías* have become hangouts for students and hipsters (see page 130). In Tlaxcala State there are Ruta del Pulque tours to visit historic *haciendas*, see how the *aguamiel* (juice) is extracted from the plant, and try a few jars of the finished product.

Tequila or Mescal?

Mexico's most famous export must be tequila, a party-starting spirit known the world over for the "tequila slammer," a drinking ritual involving salt, lemon, and a shot glass. Mexico's other famous liquor is mescal.

Technically, tequila is a mescal. To earn its name it has to be made solely from the blue agave (*agave tequilana*) and can only be produced in the states of Jalisco, Tamaulipas, Michoacan, Guanajuato, and Nayarit. Mescal, meanwhile, is made in Oaxaca, Durango, Guanajuato, Guerrero, San Luis Potosí, Tamaulipas, Zacatecas, and Michoacan from up to thirty varieties of agave. *Espadin* is the predominant species in Oaxaca, where most mescal is still produced on *palenques* (small farms) using traditional methods.

The best tequilas and mescals are made from "100 percent agave," meaning no other sugars were added during the distillation process. *Plata* (silver) is unaged tequila and is the best mixer for cocktails such as Margaritas. *Oro* (gold) gets its golden hue from a colorant and should not be confused with the superior quality *reposado* (rested), which has spent from two months to a year in oak barrels. *Añejo* (aged) is usually smoother, with subtler flavors, and has spent at least a year in oak barrels. *Extra añejo* has spent at least three years in oak.

When it comes to drinking, note that *aficionados* of tequila and mescal don't slam; they sip.

Mexico may not be famous for its wines, but some award-winning reds and whites are grown in northern Baja California. The first grapes were planted here by Jesuit and Franciscan missionaries in the 1700s and thrived in the Mediterranean-like climate. Places like Valle de Guadalupe and Valle de Santo Tomás are now a mecca for wine lovers who come to try the local chardonnays, nebbiolos, and sauvignons and tour the vineyards of top bodegas such as Monte Xanic. In August a major wine festival coincides with the *vendimia,* the annual grape harvest. Aguascalientes, Coahuila, Durango, Queretaro, Sonora, and Zacatecas also produce wines, but 90 percent of Mexican wine is produced in Baja California.

EATING OUT

Rich or poor, Mexicans love to eat out. Starting with breakfast from *taco* stalls or juice vendors, eaten on the run, and continuing with lunch from a *fonda* (small eatery) serving *comidas corridas* (set lunches), there is a vast variety of snacks available on the streets, and a huge range of restaurants serving food and drinks into the early hours.

Some visitors may be surprised, given the quality of Mexican cuisine, to find so many fast-food chains from north of the border in Mexico's cities and towns. Step into a shiny shopping mall, and the food court will be dominated by US-style restaurants or homegrown copies. However, head over to recognized restaurant districts and you'll find all types of cuisine, from Italian pizzas and pastas to high-end gourmet cuisine served in sophisticated surroundings.

Restaurant Casa de los Azulejos in Sanborns, Mexico City.

Award-winning gastronomy is not just the preserve of Mexico City, where restaurants like Pujol, Sud 777, Rosetta, and Quintonil serve up world-class tasting menus to discerning diners; trail-blazing chefs are also making their mark in other areas of the country. In 2022, the 50 Best Latin American Restaurants List, chosen by chefs, included five restaurants in Mexico City as well as Fauna and Villa Torél in Baja California, Le Chique in Cancún, Arca in Tulum, Pangea in Monterrey, and Alcalde in Guadalajara.

At weekends the local love of food extends to village squares and parks, as families and friends gather to relax with picnics and barbecues.

TIPPING
....

Mexico has a tipping culture, and many people rely on a *propina* (tip) to supplement a meager income. Some depend on them for their livelihood. Everybody who helps you out in some way will appreciate a few pesos in return, from bellboys and maids, to waiters, toilet attendants, and the boys who help pack your groceries at the supermarket.

Some cafés and restaurants add a *propina* to the bill, but generally it is up to the customer to leave 10–15 percent extra for the waiting staff, and more if service is exceptional. At food stalls on the street or in markets there is no obligation to tip.

For hotel staff, calculate tips of around US $1 and upward. Tour guides may be on very low salaries, especially Indigenous guides in remote areas, and the equivalent of a few dollars will be much appreciated. There is no need to tip taxi drivers.

If a group of mariachi musicians start serenading you at a bar and you appreciate the song, you can give them the equivalent of a few dollars, but don't feel obliged to pay for music if you didn't ask them to play. They'll soon move on to the next table.

NIGHTLIFE

You can get a drink at pretty much any time of the day or night in a Mexican *cantina, taverna*, or bar. Some places will even serve customers a free *botana* (savory snack) after a certain number of drinks. There was a time when it was frowned upon for women to swing through the cowboy-style doors into a *cantina*, and you can still see old signs on some traditional establishments refusing entry to women, minors, and uniformed soldiers.

More fun are the countless bars and pubs that spill onto the streets of most towns and cities, where you can sit at a table and watch the world go by. *Pulquerías* (bars serving *pulque*) used to be plentiful back in the days when the painter Frida Kahlo and her Bohemian buddies used to hang out in them. Today, they are worth seeking out to experience firsthand a truly pre-Hispanic Mexican beverage. Decorated in Aztec-style murals, Las Duelistas in Mexico City is a veritable shrine to *pulque* and attracts a young hipster crowd that has helped to make *pulquerías* trendy again.

Mexicans love to dance, and there are countless bars and clubs in cities and towns that have live music or DJs playing traditional Mexican music, *cumbia*, *salsa*, rock, pop, or the latest chart hits. Tourist resorts in Baja California, Acapulco, and Cancún have a year-round party scene that is particularly wild during Spring Break.

Wherever you are in Mexico, be aware that bars with flashing neon lights in out-of-the way places may be *casas de citas* (brothels).

MUSIC

Mariachi music is the soundtrack to Mexican life—the music of the serenade, the bullfight, the rodeo, the backing for the birthday song "Las Mañanitas," the highlight of a *quinceañera* party or a wedding, and the sad accompaniment for the jilted lover drinking alone. Originating in Jalisco State, mariachi is rooted in the *charro* (cowboy) traditions of the central highlands and northern border states, but has become a national expression of *mexicanidad* (Mexicanness).

But there is much more to Mexican music than mariachi. The popular tune "La Cucaracha" is a *corrida,* Ritchie Valens' rock and roll hit "La Bamba" is an adaptation of a *son jarocho* from Veracruz, and in the Huasteca region the *son huasteco* features trios playing violin, *huapangera* guitar, and the small, five-string *jarana* guitar.

Veracruz and the Yucatán have a historical connection to Cuba, and there is a strong musical tradition of *boleros* and *trova* sung by artists like the Afro-Mexican singer Toña la Negra, Los Panchos, and Armando Manzanero. In the far north the musical tradition of *corridas*, polkas from Germany, and accordion music has spawned several genres from the oom-pah-pah of *norteño* groups such as Los Tigres del Norte to the brass-heavy *cumbias*, the romantic *boleros,* and the brash *narco-corridos* of artists like Los Tucanes de Tijuana or El Komander, who have both penned songs in honor of Joaquín "Chapo" Guzmán, glorifying the gangster lifestyle of the *narcos*. An alternative version of *norteño* by electronic collective Nortec has had considerable success in Latin America and the US.

MEXICO CITY'S MARIACHI MECCA

Salon Tenampa in Mexico City's Plaza Garibaldi is a shrine to the greats of mariachi music, or *rancheras*. The bar was opened in 1925 by Juan Hernández, who was already bringing musicians from his hometown of Guadalajara to play in the capital before the mariachi boom took off in the movies in the 1940s. The walls of the Tenampa are decorated with huge paintings of mariachi greats like Pedro Infante, Jorge Negrete, José Alfredo Jiménez, Vicente Fernández, and more modern interpreters of the genre like Alejandro Fernández. Among the famous women gracing the walls are Amalia Mendoza, Lola Beltrán, and the gravel-voiced Chavela Vargas.

Customers pay about US $10 to request a song from a group of mariachis in the bar, and as the tequilas flow and the night wears on the impassioned singing and cowboy yelps grow ever louder. The classic line-up includes singer, violins, trumpets, classical guitar, *vihuela* (five-string guitar), and *guitarrón* (a large bass). Outside in the plaza, troupes of musicians dressed in sombreros and silver-studded *charro* (Mexican cowboy) outfits serenade passers-by or wait to be whisked off to weddings and parties.

In recognition of mariachi music's contribution to Mexico's culture and identity it was added to UNESCO's Intangible Cultural Heritage list in 2011.

Rock music faced state repression in the late 1960s and early '70s, as it was linked to student protests. Influential rock bands include El Tri, Caifanes, and Maná, who's known as the U2 of Mexican pop rock. The big bands of the late '90s were indie group Café Tacuba and Molotov, who combined political lyrics with punk, rap, and metal to create a sound that is still widely influential today.

Contemporary artists include Julieta Venegas, Camilo Lara, who explored electronica with the Mexican Institute of Sound, and Mexrrissey, a band that covers Morrissey songs in Spanish. Lila Downs has reinvented traditional folk songs and mariachi classics for a new generation.

CULTURAL ACTIVITIES

Mexico is a cultural melting pot that includes everything from the very traditional to the very modern. On the same day you might find yourself enjoying Aztec dance, a wild folk festival, and the rigorous disciplines of ballet or contemporary dance. Artworks range from the pre-Columbian ceramics of ancient civilizations to the sacred carvings of gilded colonial churches, the revolutionary murals of the 1930s, and the conceptual conceits of modern galleries.

Mexico City has more museums and cultural institutions than any other city in the world, and the streets are filled with buskers and street theater to complement the concerts and plays performed at the city's many cultural venues.

Museo de Bellas Artes (Museum of Fine Art) in Mexico City.

Much emphasis is placed on the work of the Mexican artist Diego Rivera. Some of his most important historical murals depicting the rich history of Mexico can be seen on the walls of Mexico City's National Palace. Rivera is also renowned for his tumultuous on-off love affair with Frida Kahlo, Mexico's most famous artist, and their lives and work can be enjoyed on a visit to the homes where they lived, which have been opened to the public. Frida Kahlo's Casa Azul (Blue House) is always swamped by visitors seeking insights into her highly personal art, but head down to Diego Rivera's personal collection of pre-Columbian art, the Museo Anahuacalli, and you will have the place to yourself. The Mexican muralists David Siqueiros and José Clemente Orozco also deserve attention, as does abstract painter Rufino Tamayo, who has a museum dedicated to his work in Mexico City.

Museum Soumaya art museum in Mexico City houses some 66,000 works of Mexican and foreign art from a period spanning over three thousand years.

CINEMA

During the Golden Era of Mexican cinema in the 1940s and '50s hundreds of movies were made in Mexico launching the careers of comedians like Cantinflas and Tin Tan, singers like Pedro Infante, and divas like Dolores del Rio. During those years Spanish director Luis Buñuel came to live and work in Mexico, producing award-winning arthouse movies like *Viridiana* and *The Exterminating Angel*, and Mexico City became the film capital of Latin America. The 1970s and '80s saw a decline and a reliance on "*sexicomedias*" and low-budget indie films to keep the industry alive as TV took over from cinema and Hollywood movies reigned at the box office.

A renaissance known as El Nuevo Cine Mexicano

(New Mexican Cinema) came in the 1990s with critically acclaimed movies such as *Como Agua Para Chocolate* (*Like Water for Chocolate*) a magical-realist romance directed by Alfono Arau, and the Gothic horror film *Cronos* by Guillermo del Toro.

In the twenty-first century, the violent but poetic *Amores Perros* (*Love's a Bitch*) directed by Alejandro González Iñárritu, and *Y Tu Mamá También (And Your Mother Too)* by Alfonso Cuarón were international hits that led to major success in Hollywood. Alfonso Cuarón went on to win an Oscar for Best Director in 2013 for Gravity, Alejandro González Iñárritu won four Oscars for *Birdman* in 2014 and three for *The Revenant* in 2015, and Guillermo del Toro took home four Oscars in 2017 for *The Shape of Water.*

Alfonso Cuarón returned to Mexico City for his 2018 movie *Roma*, an autobiographical tale of his childhood seen through the eyes of his nanny Cleo played by the untrained actress Yalitza Aparicio (see page 101). Released on Netflix, the film garnered 10 nominations and scooped up Oscars for Best Director, Best Cinematography, and Best Foreign Language Film. This film also hailed a new wave of Indigenous pride in Mexico and as a result, Aparicio, who is of mixed Mixtec and Triqui ancestry, was named one of the 100 most influential people in the world by *TIME* Magazine in 2019.

For a quick snapshot of Mexican society, watch the movies that have captured the national imagination over the years. In *Nosotros Los Nobles* (*The Noble Family*), Director Gaz Alazraki shines a scornful light on the nation's pampered rich kids, the *mirreyes*. Released in

2013, it's Mexico's biggest grossing movie. *Carmín Tropical* is a modern film noir set in the fishing village of Juchitán, in Oaxaca, which delves into the little-known world of *muxes*, men from Zapotec communities who dress as women and who have been treated as a third gender since pre-Hispanic times. Produced in 2010, *El Infierno* (*Hell*) is a black comedy by Luis Estrada that follows a migrant deported from the US who returns home only to get sucked into the seedy and violent world of the narco "El Cochiloco" (the Crazy Pig). It exposes the futility of the drug war and the chaos and corruption that drug trafficking brings in its wake.

SPORTS

The pre-Columbian civilizations of Mexico played a ritualized ball game linked to human sacrifice that is described in the Popol Vuh, a Mayan creation myth. Nowadays, when it comes to passion, pride, and personal sacrifice, the king of sports is *fútbol* (soccer).

Other popular sports are baseball and boxing. One of the greatest Mexican boxers of all time is Julio César Chávez, who won six world titles in the featherweight, lightweight, and light welterweight divisions over a twenty-five-year career, including thirteen years in which he was undefeated in eighty-seven bouts.

Soccer
It was Cornish silver miners from Camborne and Redruth who brought their love of savory pasties and addiction

to soccer to Real del Monte in Hidalgo State in the mid-nineteenth century. By 1901 the British miners had set up the first *fútbol* club in nearby Pachuca, and *pastes* (Cornish pasties with a chili kick) were firmly established as a favorite local dish. Club de Fútbol Pachuca is still one of Mexico's top teams, playing in the Liga MX against Guadalajara, Toluca, Cruz Azul, and Club América, based at Mexico City's enormous Estadio Azteca.

The Liga MX draws the largest crowds on average of any football league in the Americas and every weekend thousands of people in stadiums across the country cheer on their local teams; millions more tune in to local and international soccer matches at home, while many will head out to a bar to watch a match with friends. When they're not watching soccer, people are playing it, in five-a-side leagues or in a kick-around in the park.

Everything stops when the national side El Tri (El Tricolor) is playing. It has won the CONCACAF (North America, Central America, and the Caribbean) Gold Cup seven times since 1991.

Mexico competed in the first World Cup in 1930 and has qualified for an impressive seventeen World Cups, making it to the quarter-final in 1970 and 1986 (the years Mexico hosted the tournament).

Top goal scorers for the national side are revered as gods, like Javier "Chicharito" Hernández, who played for top European clubs Real Madrid and Manchester United, and Hugo Sánchez Márquez, who went to play for rivals Atlético Madrid and Real Madrid in Spain.

In the country that brought the world the Mexican Wave, the atmosphere in stadiums is festive and family-friendly. However, the roar of "*Eeeeeeehhh! Puto!*" every time the opposition goalkeeper takes a goal kick has not been well received abroad, earning the national side reprimands and fines from FIFA, football's governing body. Fans argue that chanting "*puto*" (male prostitute) has nothing to do with homophobia but is simply a long-held tradition. Despite numerous fines, unrepentant fans continued the chant during the national side's qualifying games for the 2022 World Cup in Qatar.

Charreria

Combining culture, tradition, costume, revolutionary history, horse riding, mariachi music, and *mezcal*, is it any wonder that *charreria* (rodeo) is the official national sport of Mexico? The *charro* (cowboy) with his broad-brimmed sombrero, short jacket, and spurs is seen as quintessentially Mexican, an image reinforced by actors from the Golden Age of Mexican cinema like Pedro Infante and Jorge Negrete, strong, silent types who sang sad *rancheras* (mariachi songs) when they weren't riding the range. The *charro* tradition is also a part of Mexico's revolutionary history and is linked to icons like Emiliano Zapata. Every September the best rodeo riders come to Guadalajara to compete in *charreadas* (tests of horsemanship) at the Mexican National Charro Championship, although there is as much art as sport involved in the roping and bull-riding competitions.

Lucha Libre

With their masks, capes, and tights, Mexico's *luchadores* look more like comic-book superheroes than professional

A *luchador* on the ropes during the annual wrestling festival in La Candelaria, Mexico City.

wrestlers, but anybody who attends a bout in Mexico City's Arena Coliseo or Arena Mexico will quickly see that the blood, sweat, and tears are real. *Lucha libre* (freestyle wrestling) evolved from Greco-Roman wrestling in the nineteenth century, but the masks and elaborate aerial maneuvers that make it such an exhilarating spectacle were adopted in the 1930s and '40s. The most famous Mexican wrestler is El Santo, a huge celebrity in the 1950s who appeared in cartoon strips and a series of movies where he saved the world from aliens and werewolves. He was even buried in his trademark silver mask.

Contests focus as much on entertainment as on sport, pitting *técnicos* (heroes) against *rudos* (villains) in battles of good against evil. *Luchadoras* (female wrestlers) have their own league, and bouts are as frenetic and bruising as the men's. Wrestlers known as *exóticos* are flamboyant gender-benders. Cassandro, the first openly gay *luchador,* is an *exótico* who has done much to challenge macho attitudes to homosexuality in the ring and in society as a whole.

Others who have used *lucha libre* to lead social protests are Super Barrio, who led a campaign in the late 1980s to highlight the plight of slum dwellers, and Fray Tormenta (Friar Storm), a parish priest who kept his orphanage afloat with the proceeds from his bouts. The 2006 Hollywood movie *Nacho Libre* is loosely based on the exploits of Fray Tormenta.

Bullfighting

Bloodthirsty and brutal as it may be, and despite growing calls for it to be banned, bullfighting is alive and well in Mexico. The Plaza México in Mexico City is the largest bullring in the world, with some 41,000 seats, although nowadays it hosts more pop concerts than *corridas* (bullfighting tournaments). The late-October-to-May bullfighting season coincides with the recess in Spain, allowing big name *toreadores* (bullfighters) to fight in Mexico. The highlights of the Feria de San Marcos in Aguascalientes are bullfights and cockfights, and the bull ring in Tijuana, Baja California, attracts tourists from the US who come to experience the cultural and ritualistic elements of the *corrida*. Animal rights campaigners have called for a nationwide ban on bullfighting, following statewide bans in Sonora in 2013, Coahuila in 2014, and Guerrero in 2015. Polls show that the majority of Mexicans would support such a move.

SHOPPING

You can find all the usual shops in Mexico's mega-malls, but for a real appreciation of the enormous range of food, shoes, clothing, household goods, toys, spiritual paraphernalia, pets, and *piñata* on sale you have to explore the country's covered markets and *tianguis,* the street markets that pop up on specific days.

Mexico City alone has dozens of local markets specializing in different goods, including the Mercado de San Juan near the center, where chefs go to buy exotic meats like crocodile and wild boar, and the Mercado de Sonora, famous for its potions, spells, and *brujos* (witches).

Handicrafts

There are loads of good *artesanías* (handicrafts) to pick up in Mexico—a legacy of the country's sophisticated pre-Columbian past, the large number of surviving Indigenous groups, and the abundance of folk artists putting a new spin on traditional designs.

Mexican mines have produced high-quality silver for thousands of years, and the mining towns of Taxco, Zacatecas, and San Luis Potosí are home to skilled silversmiths who produce fine jewelry in pre-Columbian and modern designs. When it comes to finding quality, you're better off buying from shops rather than on the street, and look out for the 925 sterling silver mark.

The papier-mâché skulls, skeletons, and masks made in Pátzcuaro, Oaxaca, and CDMX for the Día de los Muertos (Day of the Dead) celebrations are creatively creepy. Reproductions of famous Day of the Dead prints by the engraver José Guadalupe Posada are readily available, and every year brings new variations on characters like the Calavera Catrina (Skeleton Catrina).

The symbolic and highly psychedelic folk art of the Huichol, from the Sierra Madre Occidental, is rooted in ancient myths and shamanistic visions brought on by the hallucinogenic peyote cactus. The highest artistic expression of the Huichol spirit world is expressed in elaborate yarn paintings, but commercial handicrafts featuring the same symbolic designs are sold in Puerto Vallarta, Guadalajara, and San Miguel de Allende.

An example of the colorful and symbolically charged painted yarn of the Huichol.

CHAPTER SEVEN

TRAVEL, HEALTH, & SAFETY

Mexico has a good transportation infrastructure that includes well-maintained highways and toll roads; modern, air-conditioned buses traveling the main routes; and busy airports serving the major cities and tourist resorts. It may be smaller than its huge neighbors to the north, but Mexico is still one of the largest countries in Latin America and is best experienced through well-planned visits to specific destinations. Traveling around is generally cheaper than in the USA or Europe, whether you go by air, bus, or taxi. With online booking available for most flights, buses, and accommodation, it is easy to organize your trip, unless you plan to head out into the wilds. Before you travel, make sure you have adequate travel and health insurance to cover you for treatment in case of accident or illness.

FLYING

There are one hundred passenger airports in Mexico, the largest of which is Benito Juárez International Airport that serves Mexico City. There are also busy international airports in Cancún, Guadalajara, Monterrey, Tijuana, Los Cabos, Puerto Vallarta, and Mérida. Many smaller airports serve internal flights. A new airport serving Mexico City, the Felipe Ángeles International Airport, was inaugurated in March 2022 and is run by the Mexican Army.

The country's main carrier is Aeroméxico, the national flag carrier that was once state-owned but is now part of the SkyTeam alliance with Delta, Air France, and Korean Air. A host of US and European carriers compete for passengers to Mexico, and it pays to shop around.

For internal flights, new, low-cost airlines are challenging Aeroméxico Connect's dominance, including VivaAerobus and Volaris, which is now flying from Guadalajara to Texas. An internal flight can cost three or four times more than a long-distance bus fare but will save considerable time. Book in advance for the best deals and try to avoid travel during the Christmas, Easter, and summer vacations, when prices are higher and there is less availability.

BUSES

The cheapest option for both long- and short-distance travel in Mexico is to take a bus.

Hollywood often peddles the tired stereotype of poor peasants and their livestock crammed into clapped-out contraptions belching clouds of smoke as they wheeze lazily down dusty rural roads or race perilously round hairpin bends. Look hard enough in the remoter corners of Mexico and you might even come across one of these "chicken buses," as travelers have dubbed them. If you do have to take one, relax and enjoy the experience, as this kind of encounter with rural Mexican life is becoming rare.

The reality is that most major cities in Mexico have modern, air-conditioned bus stations with food fairs and free Wi-Fi where you can catch comfortable buses with onboard entertainment that depart frequently, are competitively priced, and can get you just about anywhere.

Mexico City has four bus terminals serving the north, south, east, and west of the country. In most cities and towns the central bus station is on the outskirts and is called either the Central Camionera, the Central de Autobuses, or Terminal de Autobuses.

There are three classes of long-distance bus, sometimes called a *camión* rather than an *autobús*. Top of the range and the most expensive are the executive services billed as Ejecutivo, De Lujo, or Pullman. The luxury extras include hot drinks, onboard toilets, and more comfortable seats than buses in the Primera category, which also offer reserved seats, videos, and air-con. *Segunda* (second-class) can vary in quality, may not have air-con, and will generally make more stops along the way. Direct buses will be identified as *directo* or *expreso*.

The bigger bus companies, such as Primera Plus, ADO, OCC, Omnibus de México, ETN, and others have good websites and apps where you can book online, and view timetables showing departure (*salida*) and arrival (*llegada*) times. If you can't book online, try to get a ticket at the terminal the day before you travel, especially at peak times. For general route planning and journey times, the most useful apps are Moovit and Rome2Rio.

TRAINS

Passenger train services ceased to operate in most of Mexico following privatization of railroads in the late 1990s. The few surviving rail experiences include the Chihuahua–Pacific Railway, which travels through the

"El Chepe" traveling through the Copper Canyon in northern Mexico.

Barranca del Cobre (Copper Canyon), considered one of the world's great train journeys. Less awe-inspiring, but stimulating in its own way, is the train that runs from Guadalajara through blue agave plantations to the José Cuervo tequila hacienda and distillery in Tequila, the town that gave its name to Mexico's most famous export.

RIDE THE RAILS ON EL CHEPE

With thirty-seven bridges and eighty-six tunnels, the 405-mile Ferrocarril Chihuahua–Pacífico represents a major feat of nineteenth-century engineering and is one of the last narrow-gauge railroads in North America. Known affectionately as "El Chepe," it offers an epic way to ride through the Barranca del Cobre, or Copper Canyon, a truly jaw-dropping, awe-inspiring series of roughly-cut valleys that are not only deeper than Arizona's Grand Canyon but cover a wider area.

El Chepe chugs along between Los Mochis on the Pacific coast and up through the Sierra Tarahumara to Chihuahua. Passengers can choose to stop at Creel, a base for hiking, and Divisadero, where you can try local dishes and handicrafts made by the Tarahumara, an Indigenous group native to the Sierra Madre famous for their long-distance running.

An ambitious tourist train project called the Tren Maya is under construction in the Maya region of southern Mexico that, when completed, will link the archaeological site of Palenque in Chiapas with sites in Campeche, Yucatán, and Quintana Roo, creating a 948-mile (1,525-km) circular loop around the Yucatán Peninsula. Announced in September 2018 by Mexican president-elect Andrés Manuel López Obrador, the project has been criticized for the environmental impact it will have on some of the remote forests that it is due to pass through as well as on the wildlife, especially jaguars, that live there.

DRIVING

The peak-hour gridlock, suffocating car fumes, and revved up "Chilangos," as the locals are known, are usually enough to deter newcomers from attempting to navigate Mexico City's sprawling streets from behind the wheel. Thankfully, with affordable taxis and an easy-to-use Metro system, you can spare yourself the headache.

Elsewhere in Mexico, however, such as when touring colonial towns or the archaeological ruins of the Yucatán, driving yourself makes sense and can be an enjoyable way to see the country at your own pace. It's a good idea to do your homework before setting out to make sure you know where you're going. With the aid of a good map or reliable navigation app like Waze, driving in Mexico needn't be particularly testing, though there are a couple of caveats. It's not advisable to drive at night nor pass through any hotspots that are known for criminal activity (see page 161). Wherever you travel you are likely to find that signposting is less than adequate, and that toll roads are worth the money.

It pays to give other drivers plenty of leeway, and always heed local advice before setting out.

The Roads

Outside the cities, the country's road network is very good between the main cities, and better in the north of the country than the south.

Super carreteras, or "superhighways," are the widest, at four lanes, and also the fastest. They have the least traffic and the highest tolls.

Cuotas, "tolls," are the next step down, and are cheaper to use. They range in quality and width, from four lanes to one, and you are likely to encounter more trucks and buses. Always have cash handy if taking toll roads.

Libres, or "free roads," carry the bulk of the traffic and are invariably more congested. They also run through the center of towns, and some are in bad condition, but if you are not in a hurry, they can give you a better flavor of the country than a toll road.

Distances are measured in kilometers and speed limits are 110 kmph (68 mph) on superhighways and toll roads, and 40 kmph (25 mph) in built-up areas, while many single-lane rural roads are restricted to 70 kmph (45 mph).

Fuel

Until 2017 all gas stations were run by Pemex and fuel prices were the same across the country except along the US border, where prices are closer to US prices. New filling stations run by Pemex, BP, Shell, ExxonMobil, and Oxxo have seen an improvement in services for motorists and introduced a variety of prices. Gas stations in Mexico are full service and gasoline is unleaded, with Magna, a regular 87 octane fuel, and Premium UBA, which is 91 octane. Diesel is also available. Always check the pump is set to zero before the attendant starts and ask either for *lleno* (full) or the amount of fuel you want in pesos. It's best to make sure you always have cash to hand as some gas stations do not accept card payments. In rural areas and on some highways gas stations can be far apart, so fill up where you can.

Rules of the Road

Mexicans drive on the right; seatbelts are compulsory; and it is illegal to drink and drive. Foreign drivers should acquaint themselves with road signs in Spanish and keep an eye open for speed bumps (*topes*), potholes, and wandering livestock.

The Policía Federal de Caminos, or Federal Traffic Police, can offer assistance if you break down on the highway, while in towns you can approach the Policía de Tránsito for help. Mexicans are generally wary of traffic police, who, when they stop drivers, have a reputation for coming up with infractions that require the payment of a fine (*una multa*). Be polite at all times and emphasize the fact you are a foreign visitor. If you do get a fine, you are unlikely to get a receipt for it. If you're not happy about the service you get from the police, wait until you are safely at your destination before pursuing a complaint (*una denuncia*).

Metrobus in Universidad Station in Mexico City.

URBAN TRANSPORTATION

In Mexico's towns and cities there are several ways to get around, from local buses (*camiones*) to barely regulated minivans known as *combis*, *micros*, and *colectivos*. Some are so small that you get to touch knees with the other passengers.

For Mexico City's rapid transport system, Metrobús, you pay by prepaid smartcard, but on most local buses (also known as *peseros* as the fare used to be one peso), you pay the driver when boarding or disembarking, and they will stop when asked. In Mexico City, *peseros* have been called loud, crowded, and dangerous to ride due to their blaring music and the risk of being robbed.

Outside peak times, the best way to get around Mexico City is on the Metro, the second-largest subway system in

Passengers boarding the Metro in Mexico City.

Pink and white CDMX taxi in Mexico City.

North America after New York, with twelve lines and 195 stations. Up to 5 million people a day travel on the Metro and after more than fifty years in operation the system is showing signs of wear, leading to occasional breakdowns. To reduce harassment of female passengers there is a separate pink carriage for women, usually at the end of the train.

Taxis are another cheap way to get around, and hail-a-ride platforms like Uber and DiDi offer low-fare rides compared to Mexico City's official pink and white cab fleet. To avoid problems, always take official cabs, preferably from a taxi rank, known as a *sitio*, or call a reliable taxi service and ask to be picked up.

A greener alternative for those who prefer to travel under their own pedal power, Mexico City has a tap-and-ride bike-share system called Ecobici that in 2023 had 687 docking stations and 9,300 bikes available. For an effortless glide, e-scooters from global firms like Lime and Movo are another alternative for exploring central areas of Mexico City.

WHERE TO STAY

Visitors can find almost every kind of accommodation in Mexico, from boho-chic boltholes for Hollywood A-listers in San José del Cabo, to hammocks strung up in a fisherman's shack for backpackers on a budget.

Hotels are graded from one to five stars, with six-star all-inclusive resorts in Mexico's top beach resorts in Puerto Vallarta and Cancún. Historic haciendas, mansions, and convents have their own category, and sometimes have limits on what they can offer due to preservation concerns, but give a real taste of Mexico's rich past. Hammocks and rustic beach cabanas have no stars at all, and camping is free on some beaches, but always enquire with locals first, as campers are a target for robbery in some places.

Local hotel chains include Presidente Intercontinental and Camino Real, and tend to have more character than the international chains such as Marriott and Sheraton.

Airbnb operates throughout Mexico, offering an easy way to book anything from a hipster-friendly room in Mexico City's fashionable Condesa neighborhood to a whole surf retreat in Baja California.

HEALTH

Mexico has good-quality health care and well-equipped modern hospitals offering all major treatments for those with the money to afford them. Public health care can be less reliable.

Mexicans often head to the pharmacy as a first port of call for minor ailments. Many medicines that require a prescription in other countries, including antibiotics, can be bought over the counter, and pharmacists can give medical advice. Prices for medicines are generally higher than in the US and roughly equivalent to those in the UK. If you fall seriously ill, ask for the number of an English-speaking doctor from your hotel or consulate, or ask local people for the best hospital.

Health Precautions

There are no compulsory vaccinations for visitors to enter Mexico, including for Covid-19. The one exception is if you are arriving from a country where yellow fever is present, then a vaccination certificate is required. Vaccinations against Hepatitis A and B, typhoid, diphtheria, polio, and tetanus (or a booster shot) are all recommended if you are traveling to remote rural or jungle areas. Malaria is present in the rural south of Mexico and up-country Yucatán, so precautions should be taken for visits to these areas.

The tropical sun is fierce, especially at altitude and even on cloudy days, so apply sunscreen and wear a hat. Mosquitoes come out to bite as the sun sets, so bring shirts with long sleeves and long pants, and slap on the bug repellent before they get you. Bring any prescribed medication with you, along with such items as contact lens solutions and/or a spare pair of glasses.

Natural Hazards

Altitude sickness: Symptoms include dizziness, headaches, and labored breathing. Regular stops and a gradual ascent will help you acclimatize. If symptoms persist, descend until you feel better.

Scorpions: In remote areas, or when camping in the jungle or on beaches, follow local advice and shake out your shoes before putting them on to avoid scorpion (*alacrán*) stings. If stung by a pale yellow scorpion (*alacrán güero*), seek medical attention. Always try to catch and/or photograph the scorpion for identification.

Coral: It is easy to graze against coral when snorkeling or diving, and cuts can quickly become infected if not washed out thoroughly with an antibacterial solution, vinegar, or even your own urine. Jellyfish stings will also respond to the same treatment.

Spiders: Hairy tarantulas are the villains of many a Hollywood movie, but their bite is only slightly more painful than a bee sting. The spiders to watch out for in Mexico are the black widow and the brown recluse, or fiddleback, both of which can cause serious complications, although bites are rare and anti-venom is available.

SAFETY

Mexico most often appears in the international news when there's a major drug bust or a major event of narco gang-related violence. However, despite the negative image abroad, areas of criminal activity are generally restricted to certain hotspots that can and should be avoided. See page 161 for more on these areas.

As in most major cities and popular tourist destinations, there are pickpockets, opportunists, and scam artists who make a living preying on unwary visitors. In all cases, taking sensible precautions will reduce the risk of falling victim to crime. Carjacking and highway robbery are a problem in the north of Mexico, in Sinaloa, and on remote roads in Chiapas; you should heed local warnings and avoid driving at night in these areas. A variety of strategies are employed to get cars and buses to stop, from placing obstacles in the road to posing as drivers who have broken down and need assistance. Most carjacking victims are released unharmed after their valuables have been stolen.

In an emergency or to report a crime you can call the police on 911. Officers are unlikely to speak English, but in Mexico City and resort towns there are Tourist Police who are specially trained to deal with foreign travelers.

Trust in the police is low in Mexico. A 2022 survey found that while 80 percent of people trust the Federal Police, only 56 percent trust the State Police. The Traffic Police (*Policía de Tránsito*) are the least trusted due to the prevalence of corrupt cops stopping drivers on flimsy excuses to extort a bribe (*una mordida*). If you are stopped and issued a fine (*una multa*), you should pay it at a police station, not to the officer issuing the ticket.

EXPRESS KIDNAPPING

There has been a rise in recent years of so-called "express kidnappings" (*secuestro exprés*), in which taxi passengers are held up by one or more assailants, robbed of their valuables, taken to ATMs or banks and forced to empty their accounts over a short period of time before being released.

Avoid being a target by traveling in a group, and calling a taxi service or using a ride-hailing app rather than hailing one in the street.

If you are involved in an express kidnapping, it is best to give your assailants what they want without a fight.

TIPS ON STAYING SAFE

- Travel with others. You are safer in a group.
- Leave your gold chains, diamond rings, and expensive watches at home, and keep digital cameras and cell phones out of sight.
- Don't use ATMs in the street or at night. Try to use ATMs inside banks during the day.
- Learn some Spanish. The more you can speak and understand, the better.
- Listen to the locals. Heed advice on places to avoid and don't enter poor areas of cities and towns.
- Know where you are going. Don't wander around looking lost.
- Avoid crowds. Don't travel on the Metro in Mexico City or visit crowded markets with anything you don't want to lose. Pickpockets will take advantage of the crush to relieve you of your valuables.
- Use the hotel safe. Don't walk around with all your cash, but always have something on you that you can hand over if mugged.
- Have a backup. Keep emergency bills hidden in your belt, shoes, or clothing, just in case of need.
- Scan/photograph your passport, airline ticket, and other key documents, and email yourself and your family a copy, along with relevant bank and credit card company numbers to phone and cancel cards in case of theft or loss.

HOTSPOTS TO AVOID

While most of Mexico's major tourist centers and beach resorts are generally safe, the states of Colima, Guerrero, Michoacan, Morelos, Sinaloa, Tamaulipas, and Zacatecas have all been flagged as areas to avoid due to incidents of kidnapping, extortion, homicides, people trafficking, or confrontations between the Mexican security forces and drug cartels. The once popular beach resort of Acapulco in Guerrero has been the scene of a spate of murders in recent years and travel there is not advised until the security situation improves. Night travel on buses in certain areas of the country is also not advised because of hold-ups. For the latest information, consult the US State Department's latest Travel Advisory for Mexico, which gives specific advice for each state.

CHAPTER EIGHT

BUSINESS BRIEFING

Since signing up to NAFTA in 1994, Mexico has benefited from a prolonged period of relative economic stability and growth. Sectors that have been opened to foreign investment over the last twenty years include the automotive industry, transportation, banking, and telecommunication industries, and more recently, real estate and energy, too. Tourism, which represents about 8 percent of Mexico's GDP, has bounced back fast since the Covid-19 pandemic, and tourism infrastructure and resort construction is booming along the Riviera Maya and in Baja California. The result is a diversified and sophisticated economy that is less reliant on oil revenue than it was in the past, but is still closely tied to the economic fortunes of its huge neighbor to the north.

In the industrialized north, along the US border, mega-factories known as *maquiladoras* churn out millions of vehicles every year for US firms such as Ford, General Motors, and Chrysler, as well as European and Japanese car makers such as BMW and Nissan. In 2019, Mexico was the ninth largest car producer and the fifth largest producer of auto parts in the world.

In banking the whole panorama has changed, with US banking giant CitiGroup—which owns CitiBanamex—now vying for customers with Mexico's biggest bank Banorte as well as Santander, Canada's Scotiabank, and the Spanish group BBVA, which took over Bancomer. The entry of these foreign banking giants has led to longer banking hours, easier online banking, and a greater range of credit options.

Mexico is now signed up to Free Trade Agreements covering forty-six countries in Europe, Latin America, the Caribbean, Asia, Israel, and Australasia. Many foreign companies now operate out of Mexico to take advantage of free trade access to the US market, a relationship that was reaffirmed in 2018 under the terms of the United States-Mexico-Canada Agreement (USMCA), which came into effect in 2020. By 2022, some 80 percent of Mexico's exports were to the USA.

DOING BUSINESS IN MEXICO

For several years the Mexican government has been actively courting foreign investment to offset low oil prices and increase diversification. Oil prices have increased somewhat but the panorama is far from rosy. Security costs can be higher for operating in some parts of Mexico, and there are still problems with the rule of law and corruption. In short, setting up a business in Mexico takes time. You can't just fire off a few emails and jet in to shake hands and sign a contract. Organizing meetings, finding the people you need, and dealing with unforeseen delays can be a frustrating process at times. Expect your patience and flexibility to be tested.

As elsewhere in Latin America, who you know is as important as what you have to sell, and putting the time into networking and face-to-face contact will be crucial to the success of any business venture you embark upon.

Contact the business attaché in your country's consulate in Mexico for help. They will usually have an up-to-date list of local firms that offer legal advice and who can produce and translate contracts. Local chambers of commerce can also be useful (see page 176). The key is to find people who can get you a meeting with decision-makers or other important people in an organization, or get things moving if they stall.

PERSONAL RELATIONSHIPS

Every country has its own style of doing business, and Mexico—although strongly influenced by the US management models taught at business schools—is a place where people still like to spend time on the social niceties before getting down to brass tacks.

In the past a small elite of rich families controlled the country. If you wanted to meet the decision-makers and get deals done all you needed were the right friends, or an impressive last name to signify you came from *buena gente* (good people). That concept continues to a certain extent today, and initial meetings will often ignore the business at hand and revolve around chitchat about your family, your hometown, and your impressions of Mexico.

Building personal relationships with potential business partners can be time consuming. However, trying to rush negotiations is likely to be perceived negatively, so it's important to factor in extra time for more meetings. The key is to meet people who can provide you with good recommendations and get you direct access to company chiefs and decision-makers who you would otherwise have difficulty meeting. Making a good impression, networking, spending time getting to know the right people, and keeping contacts fresh are all important for successful business in Mexico.

DRESS CODE

Despite the tropical heat in many parts of the country, the dress code in Mexico is formal at meetings and business-related social events. Mexicans set great store by what you wear, and men will typically wear dark business suits and ties at top-level meetings. Although it is not considered appropriate to wear a tie without a jacket or to remove your jacket once seated, it's fine to follow what your hosts do. For women, the same corporate uniform applies as in the US or Europe, and dresses, skirts, and trousers are all appropriate attire. Treat breakfast and lunch meetings as formal unless told otherwise, and dress appropriately for evening events or dinner, depending on the venue.

WELCOME TO SLIMLANDIA

A self-made billionaire, Carlos Slim, the son of Lebanese immigrants, was ranked by *Forbes* magazine as the richest man in the world from 2010–13, pushing Bill Gates and Warren Buffet off the top spot. His Grupo Carso conglomerate and other businesses include banking, insurance, construction, real estate, media, retail, and restaurants—some have joked that the country should be renamed Slimlandia.

The tycoon also has significant investments abroad, with a sizable stake in Saks Fifth Avenue and a significant share of the *New York Times*, after he bailed the paper out with a US $250 million loan in 2009. His wealth increased significantly after the telecommunications industry was privatized in the 1990s and he acquired the state telecoms giant Telmex, eventually incorporating it into América Móvil, which also operates Telcel, Mexico's largest cell phone provider.

One Mexican investor described Slim as Rockefeller, Carnegie, and J. P. Morgan all rolled into one, and in 2022 his net worth was estimated to be US $87 billion. In Mexico City his power and influence can be seen in the shiny modern shopping malls of the *Nuevo Polanco* district, where the Museo Soumaya, an art museum named after his late wife, opened in 2011 to house a personal art collection of 66,000 pieces.

WOMEN IN BUSINESS

Although things are changing, especially in large corporations, top managers or CEOs still tend to be men in Mexico, and macho attitudes persist at all levels in the workplace, particularly in industries like construction. Women are still employed for their looks, especially in marketing and sales roles, and casual sexism persists. Women also receive lower salaries than their male counterparts and are over-represented in the informal sector—running street stalls or food outlets—where they are able to work with their children alongside them.

However, the number of women employed at middle-management level has grown significantly over the last five years; women are increasingly overtaking their male counterparts in the number of higher degrees they are attaining, and female entrepreneurs are making their mark in a wide range of industries. However, in 2022 less than half of Mexican women of working age were participating in the labor market, compared to 76 percent for men, and on average female employees earned 16 percent less than their male coworkers, although the gender pay gap is less pronounced in larger corporations.

As a foreign woman doing business in Mexico, you are unlikely to encounter any problems but you may find some of the attitudes toward women old-fashioned, even quaint, and some of the comments you receive may border on flirtatious. The key is to keep things professional, friendly, and polite.

When meeting a Mexican woman in a business environment for the first time, as when meeting a man, a warm handshake is the best approach. At subsequent meetings, and as the relationship develops, a kiss on the cheek is typical among Mexicans.

SETTING UP A MEETING

When dealing with government bodies the process of making appointments can be formal, bureaucratic, and slow. It's best to start at your local Mexican embassy, unless you have a direct contact, and begin with a formal letter and email in Spanish. The trade attaché at your embassy should be able to help with local advice and a list of reliable contacts and suggestions for business partners, agents, and legal representatives, and Mexican agents or partners are even better, as they will be able to get you into the office where you can arrange a meeting in person.

With large businesses used to dealing with foreign companies, a direct email in Spanish is acceptable for proposing dates for a meeting, but it should be followed up by a phone call about two weeks before the meeting and another the day before, just to check that everything is on schedule. This might seem like overkill, but in Mexico, where things can change quite quickly and where businesspeople are juggling many things at the same time, you need to keep in touch and gently remind people you're coming. Use the opportunity to build a rapport.

If you want fast results you will have to travel to Mexico and meet people in person. Entrepreneurs who have spent months sending out emails from their home country without any concrete leads will find that, once in Mexico, they have a better chance of seeing results. Mexicans prefer to deal with people face to face, and once they know you personally, they will be more likely to introduce you to other business acquaintances and help to set up meetings. Part of the challenge here, as in most places, is understanding who has the power to do business with you and sign off on deals, and how you can get hold of them.

An important consideration when scheduling appointments is that Mexicans take their weekends and public holidays seriously and there is little chance of getting anything done on a Friday afternoon or during the long holiday periods around Christmas and New Year, Carnival, or Easter.

The best time for a meeting is in the morning. Depending on the size of the company, you may be invited to a breakfast meeting with several executives and decision-makers where you can discuss things over coffee and a pastry. These often act as pre-meetings and a chance to find out more about you. Don't be frustrated if you don't get down to business straight away. This is not the place to get a decision. The same holds true for lunch meetings.

Be aware that an invitation to dinner is probably down to hospitality and the thought of you staying alone in a hotel in an unknown city rather than a burning desire to do business with you there and then. The key thing is to remain professional at all times, even when out on the town. The etiquette in Mexico is for the person issuing the invitation to pay the bill. Never offer to pay just your share of the bill; this would come across as rude. Offer to pay it all, but don't insist too much if refused, as this also may cause offense. It's better to let your host pay and for you to issue the next invitation.

PUNCTUALITY

The perception persists of Mexico as the land of *mañana* (tomorrow), and in a sense it is deserved. The vagaries of traffic, and a laid-back attitude to timekeeping by some Mexicans, especially in smaller towns, can result in a late start when it comes to meetings. A foreign businessperson, however, should always arrive on time and will need to factor in potential transport delays when making plans. If you have to wait, even for an hour or so, or even reschedule a meeting for another day, this is nothing personal—just a local peculiarity that you will have to get used to. The important thing is not to get ruffled or show undue annoyance by last-minute changes and to make sure you leave room in your schedule for contingencies.

MEETINGS AND PRESENTATIONS

The formalities of a meeting usually begin with a greeting to the group of "*Buenos días*" or "*Buenas tardes*," depending on the time of day. You will be presented to each person in the room. It is typical to shake hands. (For forms of address, see page 182.)

Bring business cards written in English on one side and the other in Spanish. Any material or brochures you bring with you should also be translated into Spanish, preferably by a local translator to get the tone right, and avoid words that have different meanings in different Spanish-speaking countries.

You will also need an interpreter or intermediary/partner who can translate, even if some people in the room speak English. Generally, senior executives in large private companies speak English, but you can't guarantee it, and junior executives with key expertise pertaining to any deal may have no English at all.

When dealing with government agencies you should always bring an interpreter and have a document drawn up in Spanish with the main points of your proposal.

Presentations should also be given in Spanish, preferably with an interpreter who can convey all the subtleties of your pitch if your Spanish is not up to it. Don't be put off if there is conversation during your presentation, or if people take phone calls or leave the room while you are speaking; this is just another example of a more relaxed attitude to doing business. Questions may be asked in a very direct way, but don't take this as confrontational, and give calm, measured responses. The key again is to keep your cool and remain friendly and professional at all times.

NEGOTIATIONS

Having given your pitch and answered questions, don't

expect an immediate answer, as several more meetings will likely be needed before a deal is finalized. Very often you will be told that somebody else has to be consulted and when dealing with government agencies that is probably the case, but in private firms this could also be a polite way of saying, "We'll think about it and get back to you."

If negotiations drag on too long, however, it probably means that the Mexican business is avoiding a straight "No," in favor of subtle hints. Having local contacts more used to the subtleties of Mexican negotiations will help to interpret the responses you receive.

CONTRACTS AND LEGAL CONSIDERATIONS

Unlike the legal systems in the US and the UK, which rely on a "common-law" system of judicial precedents, Mexico has a "written code" or "civil law" legal system like the ones in France and Spain.

Mexico's laws are a combination of its national constitution, legal codes, laws laid down in federal, state, and municipal entities, and presidential decrees. With such a complicated and wide-ranging legal landscape it is advisable to seek guidance from a well-respected law firm on all legal issues pertaining to any potential business venture before going ahead.

Use a local lawyer and professional translator to draft contracts in Spanish and English and clarify any contractual issues before signing.

It's important to contact your embassy or business chamber for the latest updates on the legal status of foreign firms in Mexico, and issues of purchasing real estate along the coast and border areas, tariff exceptions, and repatriation of profits.

MANAGING DISAGREEMENT

If there is disagreement over a contract or payment, the first and best option is to try to deal with it straight away. Good local legal advice is essential, as going to court over a contract breach can be a protracted and frustrating process. The Mexican legal system is slow, judicial rulings can be unpredictable, and the judiciary is not always impartial to external influences. The best way to avoid disputes is to maintain frequent contact with Mexican business partners, which will help to build strong personal ties and flag issues before disputes arise. This may mean a closer working relationship than one would foster with a US or UK business partner and more time spent on the ground.

MANAGEMENT STYLE

The old-school company hierarchy where the boss is the boss, and several levels of management are layered one upon another to create a classic pyramid structure, is still the norm in Mexico. Formality and the use of titles is fairly widespread. At first meetings expect to start with *Señor* (Sir) and *Usted* (the formal singular form of "you") and only switch to a less formal *tú* (informal singular form) if the person you are addressing drops the formalities.

It is typical for an engineer to be addressed as Ingeniero, a university graduate as Licenciado, and a businessman with a master's degree as Doctor. Very often the title will be included on a business card. Foreign businesspeople will not be expected to use these terms, but they do give an insight into the pecking order in a company.

A foreign businessperson managing Mexican staff will be expected to act as a boss and maintain a certain distance with staff, while exhibiting enough empathy for them to be able to express their concerns.

Mexico has strict labor laws, and foreign managers will need to be up to speed with the specific prohibitions on outsourcing and per-hour contracts as well as maternity provisions, disciplinary procedures, and how to terminate employment.

DEALING WITH RED TAPE

For the uninitiated, dealing with government entities can involve hours waiting in line or time-consuming and frustrating phone and email communication. One way to speed things up is to work with local partners, business associations, or reputable agencies who already have contacts and can cut down the time it takes to negotiate the necessary red tape. For importing or exporting goods through customs, a trusted local contact is essential, and local agents are a requirement for dealing with the government.

ORGANIZATIONS THAT CAN HELP

The US Commercial Service has offices in Mexico City, Guadalajara, and Monterrey and produces a regularly updated Country Commercial Guide aimed at assisting US companies and individuals interested in investing in Mexico with key information on commercial opportunities and trade events.

The UK Department for International Trade (DIT) has offices at the British Embassy in Mexico City, Monterrey, and Guadalajara and can advise UK businesses that want to export to or import from Mexico.

You should also approach established business associations, which can provide up-to-date information on the business climate and the market, and steer you toward reliable local partners and reputable legal firms. In Mexico City, these include the American Chamber of Commerce of Mexico, and the British Chamber of Commerce.

CORRUPTION

Mexico has a challenging corruption problem, particularly in relation to the judiciary, the police, and public officials, and in areas where criminal gangs are active and extortion is widespread. The country has consistently scored badly on Transparency International's Corruption Perceptions Index, where in 2021 it ranked 124 out of 180 countries. Ordinary Mexicans are tired of the corruption and impunity that blight their lives and have called for greater financial transparency from public officials and corporations. President Obrador came to power in 2018 with a vigorous anti-corruption campaign and installed a new special prosecutor for corruption, but bribery cases are slow to proceed and little concrete action has been taken. Foreigners doing business in Mexico should steer clear of any individual or company offering a shortcut to official procedures through any form of inducement, whether financial or in kind.

GIFT GIVING

When first meeting potential clients in Mexico you are not expected to bring a gift, but bringing something typical from your country—candy, shortbread, or a bottle of wine or whiskey picked up in Duty Free, or an illustrated book of your city or country—can act as a good icebreaker. Gifts and treating clients to hospitality are not illegal in Mexico, and many Mexican businesses will send hampers or small gifts to clients and customers at Christmas, or to celebrate an anniversary. However, it is best not to give expensive gifts like Rolex watches or gold pens, which could be misinterpreted as bribes. Some companies, particularly large multinationals operating in the country, do not allow staff to accept gifts for the same reason.

CHAPTER NINE

COMMUNICATING

LANGUAGE

There is no official language in Mexico. Instead, the Mexican constitution recognizes Spanish and no less than sixty-three Indigenous languages as national languages. That said, Spanish is the language of government and is spoken as a first language by some 95 percent of the population. Even in the few areas where Indigenous groups maintain their own languages as a first language, most people there will speak and understand Spanish, too.

The Spanish spoken in Mexico is known as *castellano,* referring to the language spoken in the Spanish region of Castile in central Spain. However, the accent you hear in Mexico differs from the Spanish you hear in Madrid in several ways. First, there is no lisp on the letters *c* and *z,* so *cerveza* (beer) sounds like *sir-vay-sir*. Second, there is a singsong accent to Mexican Spanish, most noticeable in central states like Jalisco, which is an echo of the ancient Aztec tongue Nahuatl. Then there are the words and phrases particular to Mexico, many of them rooted in the country's pre-Hispanic cultures such as Nahuatl, Maya, and Purépecha. Even a cursory glance at the map shows the prevalence of Indigenous place names. As the Spanish conquistadors encountered creatures and foods they had no names for they added them to the language. While *aguacate* (avocado, from the Aztec *ahuacatl*), *tomate* (tomato, from *tomatl*), and *chile* (chili pepper, from *chilli*) entered the universal lexicon, many other words remained only in Mexico. So when hipsters in Mexico City invite you to meet their *cuates* (pals) to drink some *pulque* (fermented cactus sap beer), they are using Aztec words.

Speaking Spanish

Every child educated in Mexico receives some schooling in English, and many Mexicans have spent time in the US or have family members living there. However, apart from people living on the US border, those employed in the tourist industry, and well-heeled sophisticates, most Mexicans you meet on your travels can only muster a few words or phrases along the lines of "How are you?", "What is your name?", and "Where are you from?"

With that in mind, the more Spanish you can learn before you arrive in Mexico, the better. Not only will you be able to ask for things and understand the replies, but you will also find it easier to make meaningful contact with the people you meet. Any attempt you make to speak Spanish will be appreciated, from a simple greeting like *"Hola!"* to a local expression like *"Que onda, güey?"* ("What's up, dude?").

Learn a few phrases like "*Sabroso, gracias!*" ("Tasty, thanks!"), to show your appreciation of food at dinner, or "*chido*" ("cool"), which might raise a smile.

If you plan to spend longer in the country there are good schools teaching Spanish to foreigners in Mexico City, Guadalajara, Monterrey, Oaxaca, Mérida, Puerta Vallarta, and expat hangouts like Puebla and San Miguel de Allende. Some schools offer homestays with a Mexican family, which is a great way to fast-track your Spanish and get real insight into the food, culture, and daily life of the country.

Other Languages

The sixty-three Indigenous languages recognized by the state in Mexico include Nahuatl, with 1.5 million speakers, Yucatec Maya, with about 750,000 speakers, and Mixtec, with some 425,000 speakers. In total, out of the 10 million Mexicans who identify as belonging to an Indigenous group, only 6.5 million speak an Indigenous language. Some languages have so few speakers that they are on the verge of extinction, although much is being done to revive Indigenous cultures and customs, and speaking the language is one of the criteria for access to government aid programs. It is estimated that 130 distinct languages have been lost since the violent conquest of Mexico by Spain and the subsequent attempt to unify the country under one language following independence in 1821.

MANNERS AND GREETINGS

Good manners and respect for others are very important in Mexico. When entering a shop or office people will say to those present, "*Buenos días*" or "*Buenas tardes.*"

To show respect, address people as *Señor/Señora/Señorita*, and the elderly as *Don/Doña* with their first name. If you don't know the marital status of a young woman, use *Señorita* and let her correct you.

When being introduced it is customary to say "*Mucho gusto*" ("Pleased [to meet you]"), or "*Es un placer conocerle*," or simply "*Un placer*" ("It's a pleasure"), followed by your first name.

In restaurants or at dinner people say "*Buen provecho*" ("Enjoy your meal") to other diners.

TALKING LOCAL

Textbook Spanish will help you get by in Mexico, but to get under the skin of the country and fit in with new friends a few typical words and phrases can go a long way. Always use slang expressions with a certain caution and assess your audience before you use them. Not all Mexicans use the same expressions, and a word that provokes mirth in northern Mexico might cause offense in the Yucatán.

"Chilangos," as the residents of Mexico City are called, have a reputation for the liveliest street slang. For a flavor of how impenetrable Chilango can sound to the untrained ear (imagine a Midwesterner trying to decipher Cockney rhyming slang), listen to Café Tacuba's version of Jaime

Lopez's song "Chilanga Banda," which starts: "*Ya chole chango chilango. Que chafa chamba te chutes. No checa andas de tacuche. Y chale con la charola.*" ("That's enough Mexico City monkey boy, your job is really lame, you don't look good in a uniform, even less with your official badge.")

Caguama	40 oz bottle of beer
Carnal	Buddy, bro
Chela	Beer
Chido	Cool
Fresa	Snob, stuck-up, preppy
Güey	From the word *buey* (ox); it means "dude" in the expression: "*Que onda, güey?*" (What's up, dude?)
Híjole!	Wow! Whoa! Expression of surprise
Órale!	"Let's go!" Used in the north
"Órale, *vato*?"	(What's up, dude?)
Padre	Cool. *Padrisimo/a* (super cool)
Mande?	Perhaps the Mexican expression you will hear most; it means the equivalent of "Can I help you?"
Naco	Low-class, cheap, tasteless. Taken from Totonaco (the Indigenous group), this pejorative term shows up Mexico's racial and class prejudices
No manches!	No way! You're kidding! A politer version of "*No mames!*" Often combined with *güey*

SPEAK LIKE AN AZTEC

The Aztec Empire might have come to a bloodthirsty end with the siege of Tenochtitlán and the conquest of Mexico by the Spanish, but the language of the empire, Nahuatl, lives on in everyday speech. This is one of the features of Mexican, as a language, that sets it apart from the Spanish spoken in Spain and other Latin American countries:

Spanish	Aztec	English
Cacahuate	*Tlacucahuatl*	Peanut
Chamaco	*Camahuac*	Boy
Chapulin	*Chapulin*	Grasshopper
Chicle	*Chictli*	Gum (chewing gum)
Chile	*Chilli*	Chili pepper
Chocolate	*Xocoatl*	Chocolate (bitter water, in Aztec)
Coyote	*Coyotl*	Coyote
Cuate	*Cuatl*	Friend (literally, twin)
Elote	*Elo-tl*	Corn on the cob
Escuincle	*Itzcuintli*	Small child (literally, hairless pre-Columbian dog)
Guacamole	*Ahuaca-molli*	Avocado sauce
Guajolote	*Guajalote*	Turkey
Mecate	*Mecatl*	Rope
Nopal	*Nopalli*	Prickly pear (edible cactus paddle)
Ocelote	*Oceloti*	Ocelot
Tecolote	*Tecolotl*	Owl
Zopilote	*Tzopilotl*	Vulture

HUMOR

Clever wordplay, a creative use of puns, and earthy double meanings are key elements of Mexican humor. Movie legend Mario Moreno Reyes, better known as Cantinflas, was a great slapstick artist with instinctive comic timing, who typically played the underdog, the *mestizo* country boy in the big city who got by on his wits and a fast tongue alone. The true power of his performances came from his ability to tie up his onscreen rivals—especially pompous authority figures—in comic knots. Cantinflas had the common touch, the humor of the *barrio*, where verbal dexterity is highly prized. You find the same humor in the songs of Chava Flores and in the hugely successful TV show "*El Chavo del Ocho*," created by the much loved comedian, actor, and writer Roberto Gómez Bolaños, whose stage name, Chesperito, means "Little Shakespeare." Another iconic figure of Mexican cinema is Germán Valdés, or Tin Tan, whose comedy came in part from mixing Mexican slang with the "Spanglish" used by Mexican Americans.

Jokes in Mexico often hinge on double meanings, known as *albur*, which can have sexual connotations. Affectionate abuse or banter that employs *albures* is typical among friends. There are even albur competitions, like verbal fencing matches, where contestants take it in turns to come up with witty put-downs until one of them is unable to conjure up a coherent reply.

While Mexicans will find comedy in every situation, and are quick to mock, they are sensitive to foreigners making fun of them or of anything they hold dear. By all means join in with the joshing and take the banter on the chin with a smile, just don't make a joke about the Mexican football team or the Virgin of Guadalupe.

BODY LANGUAGE

In general, Mexicans are not as animated as Argentinians or Italians when speaking, but they do use their hands to illustrate a point, and it's important to understand the gestures they use. It can be considered rude or aggressive to beckon to somebody with the fingers pointing upwards, like a cop directing traffic. Mexicans do it with the palm facing downward and the fingers pointing down.

To indicate that someone is being stingy or tight-fisted, it's typical to bend the arm and tap the elbow. From this you get the expression "*No seas codo*" ("Don't be elbow"), which means don't be cheap, get your wallet out.

Some gestures can be misinterpreted and should be avoided. In the US it is not uncommon to see people tapping or thumping the heart with the fist to show respect, as in the hip-hop gesture of "Peace, out"—but in Mexico it means you are indicating, and not in a pleasant way, that somebody is gay.

PERSONAL SPACE

Mexicans don't have the same strict rules on personal space that you find in some countries. They are happy to get up close, and are more hands-on when meeting. In a formal setting, men will shake hands as in the US or Europe, and you can expect a back slap or a bear hug from friends. The etiquette between women, or between a man and a woman, is a single kiss on the right cheek. This is not a romantic kiss, just a touch of the cheeks, or an air kiss. A casual wave could be seen as standoffish.

THE MEDIA

The Mexican media scene is opening up to greater competition but is still dominated by old giants like Televisa, the biggest media conglomerate in Latin America and also the largest producer of telenovelas (soap operas) and other Spanish-language content in the world.

An area of great concern is the amount of violence that journalists face. Reporters Without Borders (RSF) has described Mexico as the most dangerous country in the Western Hemisphere for journalists. More than a hundred and fifty media professionals have been murdered since the year 2000, and journalists across the country who investigate crime or corruption face daily intimidation and harassment by drug cartels or public officials who want to silence them. In 2022, Mexico scored 47.57 on RSF's Press Freedom Index, a decline from 53.29 the previous year. This ranks Mexico as one of the worst countries for freedom of the press in Latin America and the Caribbean.

Television

The two big players in Mexican TV are media giant Televisa and TV Azteca, which have two national channels each and broadcast a daily diet of news, talk, and gossip, game and reality shows, and sports, as well as US programs, such as cartoons, sitcoms, and dramas, dubbed into Spanish. The government also runs two channels that focus on Mexican music, arts, and culture.

Increasingly Mexicans in the big cities are watching their TV via satellite or cable from companies like Cablevision, SkyTV, or DirecTV, which offer movie channels and a variety of English-language news, sports, and entertainment from the US, Canada, and the UK. The arrival of streaming services such as Netflix, offering instant access to the latest TV series and movies, has shaken up the local market as more Mexicans now opt to get their TV fix online.

Radio

Mexico has the largest network of Spanish-language radio stations of any country in Latin America, and radio is still an important source of news for rural communities. Every kind of Mexican music can be heard on these stations, from *norteño* and *banda* to mariachi, *rock en español, boleros*, pop, electronica, and the latest US chart hits. Many churches and evangelical groups also operate radio stations to spread their message, and Indigenous groups have stations that broadcast in Maya, Nahuatl, and Mixtec.

Newspapers

Newsstands in Mexico are often well-stocked and offer a good variety of the printed newspapers and magazines available. Newspapers with good national and international coverage include *El Universal*, *El Economista*, *El Financiero*, *El Nacional*, and *El Sol de Mexico*. *Reforma* is considered a good newspaper for a critical analysis of events in Mexico, as is the weekly magazine *Proceso* and the left-wing daily *La Jornada*. Less serious, and certainly less sensitive, sensationalist tabloids such as *El Gráfico* feature lurid cover photos of semi-clad celebrities or shocking images of crime or accident scenes aimed at attracting attention on newsstands. In addition, hundreds of newspapers serve regional markets and individual towns and cities, some run by large conglomerates, others by independent editors.

English-Language Publications

As mentioned, there are currently more than 1.6 million US citizens who live in Mexico—the largest concentration of US expats in the world. It is no surprise then that US publications are easy to find in Mexico's big cities, though some will be a day old, as will British papers. The *International Herald Tribune* and the *New York Times* can be picked up at newsstands or in chain restaurants such as Sanborns. Weekly international news magazines such as *TIME*, *Newsweek*, *The Economist*, and a wide variety of lifestyle magazines are also available.

Based in Mexico City, *The News* is an English-language newspaper published from Monday to Friday and available at newsstands in touristic and upscale areas of the city. It can also be accessed online.

Places with large expatriate populations from the US and Canada have their own daily and weekly publications, such as the *Guadalajara Reporter* or the *Ojo del Lago* ("Eye of the Lake") in the expat haven of Chapala, in Jalisco State. In San Miguel de Allende there is a weekly paper with a calendar of local events called *Atención.* Others include the *Yucatán Times* in Mérida and the *Mexico News Daily* in Puerto Vallarta.

MAIL

Main post offices (*oficinas de correos*) are open from 8:00 a.m. to 8:00 p.m. Monday to Friday, and from 8:00 a.m.to 3:00 p.m. on Saturdays. The postal service is generally slow and unreliable, especially when sending letters or parcels abroad, or receiving them from abroad. Instead, Mexicans rely on the many private local courier services or international couriers such as DHL, FedEx, and UPS. If you just want to send a postcard home there are red and yellow mailboxes in large hotels, on the streets, and at airports.

CELL PHONES AND SIM CARDS

While landlines offer cheaper rates for calls, it can be a lengthy process to have one installed, especially in rural areas, so many Mexicans rely on cell phones to communicate. Data from 2023 showed that there were 119.8 million cellular connections in Mexico that year, indicating that many Mexicans have more than one line.

The most popular contract and pay-as-you-go providers are TelCel, AT&T, Movistar, and Virgin Mobile, and increased competition has seen user prices fall. TV Azteca's phone and Internet firm Izzi has also entered the market with cheap contracts for basic services. Depending on the provider, most Mexican contracts bill calls to cell phones in Mexico, the USA, and Canada at the local rate. 4G is the same as anywhere, and to use a local SIM card in a US or European smartphone, the phone must be unlocked.

USEFUL TELEPHONE NUMBERS

Operator services 040

Country code 52

City Codes

Guadalajara 33

Mexico City 55

Monterrey 81

Cancún 998

Mérida 999

Emergency

Police, Fire, Ambulance 911

INTERNET AND SOCIAL MEDIA

After Brazil, Mexico has the biggest Internet market in Latin America, with more than 97 million users in 2023. Since the opening of the telecommunications sector in 2013, Mexicans have been able to access the Internet in a variety of ways. Greater competition and lower prices have driven rapid growth in mobile access, and many cable companies now offer home broadband, telephone, and TV packages. While Wi-Fi is available in many hotels, restaurants, and cafés, it is not always free. Visitors to the country will find that Wi-Fi is not as widespread as in many other Latin American countries, especially in rural areas.

While the use of cell phones and laptops tapping into Wi-Fi services has reduced the popularity of the old-school Internet café, in some remote villages you can still find places charging students to do their homework, play video games, or chat online.

Social media is hugely popular in Mexico, with almost as many registered Facebook members as there are Internet users. WhatsApp is the most popular messaging app locally and is used by Mexicans of all generations. Facebook is the most popular social media app in Mexico, followed by Instagram, TikTok, Twitter, and Telegram. The rise of TikTok is driven by younger users, while older users prefer sticking to Facebook and video sharing sites like YouTube. Among social media users, only 4 percent of those aged over 65 use them regularly.

Strikingly perhaps, according to DataReportal, a total of 34 million Mexicans were reported to not be using the Internet at all in 2023, meaning that roughly a quarter of the population continue to carry out their lives entirely offline.

CONCLUSION

Mexico is one of those countries that people feel they know because of the oft-repeated stereotypes of Mexican people, music, and food portrayed in Hollywood movies, TV shows, and magazines. As we have tried to show, the reality is much more complex and nuanced. Mexicans don't just sit in the shade waiting for *mañana*. People work hard to get ahead; they believe strongly in education, and as a result have built one of the most powerful economies in Latin America.

There is *machismo*, but much is being done to improve gender equality and further the rights of the LGBTQ community. There is still a violent drug war being played out in the country, especially in the states along the long US border, but it's a war that rarely touches tourists and the safety tips outlined in Chapter 7 should help to minimize the risk.

As we've seen, some stereotypes do have a grain of truth in them: Mexicans put family first, and will happily drop everything to celebrate a folk festival with the religious zeal and Bacchanalian gusto it deserves. They love mariachi music, and it touches their soul when the trumpets begin to play and familiar songs are sung. Their love for the traditional does not preclude a love for the new, as illustrated by the vibrant pop, rock, and electronica scene, and many enjoy *cumbia*, the oom-pah-pah of *norteño,* as well as chart hits from north of the border.

Mexican food and drink are also remarkably varied and you don't have to go far in Mexico to find tasty street food that is fiery with chilis, while tequila is the tipple of choice all over the country. You'll also soon find out that Mexicans don't just stick a wedge of lime in their beer—they pour it into a large glass with chili powder around the rim, add the juice of squeezed limes, ice, and clam juice, and call it a *chelada* or a *michelada*. And they don't slam tequila with salt and lemon—they sip it as if it were a fine brandy.

Most of the food you find in Mexico is not searingly hot. Rather, it's so diverse that you could take weeks exploring the mouth-watering offerings at just one of the maze-like covered markets in Mexico City, and still have only a slim idea of the many regional specialties that make travel around the country so gastronomically rewarding. The true magic of Mexico is that it continually serves up surprises.

Whatever your reason for visiting Mexico, we hope that this book will give you the confidence to delve a little more deeply into the culture and way of life of this dynamic country and to discover for yourself the warmth, vibrancy, and friendship of its people.

FURTHER READING

Azuela, Mariano. *The Underdogs*. New York: Random House, 2002.

Cervantes, Fernando. *Conquistadors*. Penguin Books, 2021.

Christenson, Allen J. *Popol Vuh: The Sacred Book of the Maya*. Norman, Oklahoma: University of Oklahoma Press, 2007.

Cortés, Hernán. *Letters from Mexico*. New Haven, Connecticut: Yale University Press, 2001.

Díaz, Bernal. *The True History of The Conquest of New Spain*. Indianapolis: Hackett Publishing, 2012.

Harrison, John. *1591: A Journey to the End of Time*. Swansea: Parthian Books, 2015.

Herrera, Hayden. *Frida: A Biography of Frida Kahlo*. New York: Harper Perrenial, 2000.

Leon Portilla, Miguel. *The Burning Spears: The Aztec Account of the Conquest of Mexico*. Boston: Beacon Press, 2006.

Lida, David. *First Stop in the New World: Mexico City*. New York: Riverhead Books, 2009.

MacDougall, Christopher. *Born to Run: A Hidden Tribe, Superathletes, and the Greatest Race the World Has Never Seen*. New York: Vintage Books, 2011.

Paz, Octavio. *The Labyrinth of Solitude, The Other Mexico, and Other Essays on Mexico*. New York: Grove Press, 1994.

Rainsford, Catriona. *Urban Circus: Travels With Mexico's Malabaristas*. London: Bradt, 2013.

Rulfo, Juan. *Pedro Páramo*. London: Serpents Tail Publishing, 2000.

—. *The Burning Plain*. Austin: University of Texas Press, 1971.

Theroux, Paul. *On The Plain Of Snakes: A Mexican Journey*. Penguin Books, 2020.

Thomas, Hugh. *The Conquest of Mexico*. London: Harvill Press, 2004.

Townsend, Camilla. *Fifth Sun: A New History of the Aztecs*. Oxford University Press, 2021.

Wright, Ronald. *Time Among the Maya: Travels in Belize, Guatemala and Mexico*. Eland Publishing, 2020.

USEFUL APPS

Travel and Transportation

ADO The ADO bus network is one of the cheapest and safest ways to get around Mexico. On the app you can check timetables, book seats and get discounts on journeys.

Atlas Turístico de México An app and website that covers the whole country with maps and routes, as well as information on destinations and attractions.

DiDi The Chinese ride hailing app became popular during the pandemic and is now the main rival to Uber.

Ecobici An app to navigate the bicycle rental system in Mexico City, with maps showing available bike hubs.

inDriver Another taxi app popular in Mexico. It allows you to negotiate a price with the driver, but you have to pay in cash.

Moovit A one stop route-planning app.

TheCity.mx A comprehensive guide to Mexico City.

Uber The popular ride-hailing app doesn't cover the whole country and drivers are restricted from pick-ups and drop-offs at some airports, but where the app does work it can cut journey costs considerably.

Food and Shopping

Rappi More than a fast-food service, the Colombian delivery app can be used to deliver groceries from a supermarket or medicine from a pharmacy. Food delivery alternatives include **UberEATS** and **SinDelantal**

Walmart One of the largest retailers in Mexico, Walmart has a useful app that adds a delivery charge based on distance and how soon you want your groceries.

Communication

WhatsApp Mexico's most-used messaging app.

Google Translate A must-have tool for translating words and phrases as well as signs and text that you point your phone at.

Duolingo This language learning app can teach you the basics for communication with short lessons.

PICTURE CREDITS

INDEX

Acknowledgments

I would like to dedicate this book to my beloved father, Derek Maddicks, who left us too soon in the midst of the Covid-19 epidemic, but who lives on in the hearts of all who knew him. Thanks also to my son Francisco Maddicks, a mini Mexicophile, who inspires me to spread the word about the wonders of Latin America that we encounter on our research trips.